AKIESHA N. ANDERSON
Former UCLA Law Admissions Officer

Anderson
ADMISSIONS ACADEMY

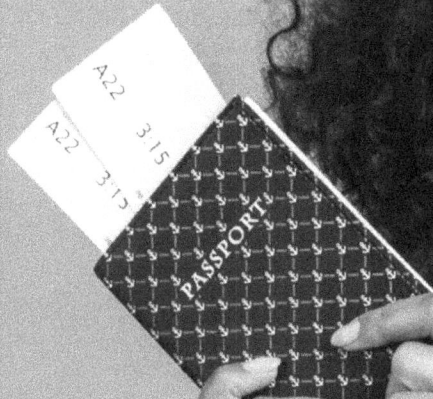

PASSPORT

A22 3.15
A22 3.15

your
ticket in
(to law school)
an insider's guide to gaining
a competitive advantage
while navigating the law
school admissions process

BONUS
Also contains 50+ sample
documents from
underrepresented students
including LORs, personal
statements, and more!

DEDICATION

To my handsome and supportive husband who encourages and inspires me to chase my dreams. Also, to my clients and supporters on Instagram (@AskAkiesha) that support the work that I do, and my efforts to diversify the legal profession by offering fiscally accessible products and services.

Table of Contents

Chapter 1: Perfecting Your Application Package (Finding Opportunities to Stand Out in a Good Way) _____ *8*

The CAS Report _____ **9**
The CAS Report: Law School Summary _____ 10
The CAS Report: Transcripts _____ 14
The CAS Report: Writing Sample _____ 15
The CAS Report: Letters of Recommendation _____ 17

The EAPP _____ **23**
The EAPP: Application _____ 24
The EAPP: Personal Statement _____ 25
The EAPP: Diversity Statement _____ 31
The EAPP: Resume _____ 34
The EAPP: Why XYZ School Essay _____ 36

Addenda _____ **39**
Addenda: GPA / Grade Explanations _____ 40
Addenda: LSAT Explanations _____ 42
Addenda: Character & Fitness Explanations _____ 43

Chapter 2: Finding the Right School for You! _____ *47*

Deciding on Where to Apply _____ **48**
Shooting Your Shot the Right Number of Time – Applying to the Right Number of Law Schools _____ 49
Creating Your Law School List _____ 49
Identifying Your Safety, Target, and Dream Schools _____ 52
A Final Note on Enhancing Your Odds of Being Liked by a Law School _____ 58

Chapter 3: I've Applied – Now What? _____ *61*

Negotiating Scholarships _____ **64**

Deciding Where to Place a Seat Deposit _____ **65**

Navigating the Waitlist _____ **66**

Applying as a Transfer Applicant _____ **72**

Pros of Transferring _____ 72
Cons of Transferring _____ 73

Appendix A: Sample Law School Report _____ **76**

Appendix B: Sample Law School Writing Sample _____ **78**

Appendix C: LOR Template _____ **82**

Appendix D: LOR Samples _____ **84**
Sample One: Professional LOR (Above Average) _____ 85
Sample Two: Academic LOR (Stellar!) _____ 88
Sample Three: Professional LOR (Average) _____ 90
Sample Four: Professional LOR (Average) _____ 93
Sample Five: Professional LOR (Stellar!)_____ 94
Sample Six: Professional LOR (Stellar!)_____ 97
Sample Seven: Professional LOR (Above Average)_____ 101

Appendix E: Personal Statement Samples _____ **103**
Sample One: Future Civil Rights Attorney _____ 104
Sample Two: Future Technology Law Attorney _____ 105
Sample Three: Future Federal Prosecutor_____ 108
Sample Four: Future Public Interest Attorney _____ 110
Sample Five: Future JAG_____ 111
Sample Six: Future Business Law Attorney _____ 114
Sample Seven: Future Legislative Attorney _____ 115
Sample Eight: Undecided Law Path _____ 118
Sample Nine: Future Business Attorney_____ 120
Sample Ten: Future Children's Rights Attorney_____ 122
Sample Eleven: Future Criminal Defense Attorney _____ 124
Sample Twelve: Undecided Law Path_____ 126
Sample Thirteen: Undecided Law Path _____ 128
Sample Fourteen: Future Human Rights Attorney _____ 129
Sample Fifteen: Future Prosecutor _____ 132
Sample Sixteen: Future Immigration Law Attorney_____ 134
Sample Seventeen: Future Civil Rights Attorney _____ 136
Sample Eighteen: Future Juvenile Justice Attorney ____ 138
Sample Nineteen: Future Criminal Defense Attorney_____ 140
Sample Twenty: Future Civil Rights Attorney_____ 142
Sample Twenty-One: Future Criminal Defense Attorney_____ 143

Sample Twenty-Two: Future Public Interest Attorney _____ 145
Sample Twenty-Three: Future Intellectual Property (IP Law) Attorney _____ 148
Sample Twenty-Four: Future Environmental Law Attorney ___ 150
Sample Twenty-Five: Future Civil Rights Attorney _____ 152
Sample Twenty-Six Future Entertainment Law Attorney _____ 154

Appendix F: Diversity Statement Samples _____ **157**
Sample One: Growing Up Biracial _____ 158
Sample Two: Growing Up Low-Income and With Parents that Immigrated to the Country _____ 160
Sample Three: Helping Dad Navigate the Legal System _____ 162
Sample Four: Passion for Dismantling the School-To-Prison Pipeline _____ 164
Sample Five: Navigating Microaggressions in the Workplace __ 165
Sample Six: Being a Queer, Black Woman Teacher _____ 166
Sample Seven: Being a [Former] Black Republican _____ 168
Sample Eight: Growing up Low-Income & Balancing Work and School _____ 170
Sample Nine: Growing up in a Drug & Crime Infested Community _____ 171
Sample Ten: Growing up Poor, Queer, in the Hood, and with an Incarcerated Parent _____ 173

Appendix G: Resume Sample _____ **175**

_____ **176**

Appendix H: Why XYZ School Essay Samples _____ **178**
Sample One: Why NYU Essay _____ 179
Sample Two: Why Michigan Essay _____ 180
Sample Three: Why Berkeley Essay _____ 181

Appendix I: Academic Addenda Samples _____ **183**
Sample One: Being First Gen & Working Throughout College _ 184
Sample Two: Family Experiencing Bankruptcy & Falling Sick _ 184
Sample Three: Being First Gen & Struggling First Semester __ 185
Sample Four: Being First Gen & Commuting Home Regularly 186
Sample Five: Having an Undiagnosed Learning Disability ____ 187

Appendix J: LSAT Addenda Samples _____ **188**

Sample One: An 11-point increase over multiple exams 189
Sample Two: Improving after taking the test cold turkey 189
Sample Three: Score decreased significantly 189
Sample Four: Taking the exam after experiencing a death in the family 190

Appendix K: Sample Character & Fitness Questions 191
Criminal Disclosures: 192
Academic Disclosures: 192

Appendix L: Character & Fitness Addenda Samples 193
Sample One: Charged with disorderly conduct 194
Sample Two: Charged with burglary 194
Sample Three: Threatening a roommate 195
Sample Four: Traffic Offenses 196

Appendix M: Applicant Profile Grids (How to Find Them) 197

Appendix N: Application Status Check Sample Email 199

Appendix O: LOCI Sample Email 201

Chapter 1: Perfecting Your Application Package (Finding Opportunities to Stand Out in a Good Way)

Oftentimes applicants feel a need to do something *extra* to help them stand out. This chapter will go over some of the do's and don'ts as it relates to that. While there are certainly some small and subtle things that applicants can do to greatly enhance their odds of being liked by an admissions committee, in my experience, most grand gestures tend to backfire or not land well for candidates. This chapter will go over some tips, tricks, and insider advice for enhancing each part of your application.

For a more in-depth explanation of each part of the law school application, check out my prior book entitled *Applying While Black (or Brown): Foundational information that minority, first generation, and low-income students need to know as they begin their law school application journey.* Unlike that book, this book assumes that you are already very familiar with all the parts of a law school application. Because of that familiarity, here I simply discuss things to be aware of to ensure that law school admissions committees are most likely to view your materials in the most favorable light possible.

The CAS Report

Let's start with the CAS Report and then go to the EAPP. As discussed in more depth in *Applying While Black (or Brown)*, your CAS Report contains your LSAT scores, an academic summary, your transcripts, your LSAT writing sample, and your letters of recommendation. Because these are mostly materials put together on your behalf and provided to schools directly by LSAC, there is often little that you can do to make these items unique or different from the other applicants you're competing against. Nevertheless, there are still some things worth knowing to help ensure that the way a school interprets everything provided in your CAS Report is favorable to you.

The CAS Report: Law School Summary

The first thing that schools will typically see when they open your CAS Report is a "Law School Summary" that I like to refer to as an academic summary. This looks similar to what is provided in Appendix A. As you'll see, there is quite a bit of information contained on this page. Your home state, age, major, names of all colleges you attended, information about any graduate degrees pursued, your year-by-year academic performance, any academic accolades or sanctions, your LSAT performance, how others of your graduating institution performed academically and on the LSAT in comparison to you, your school-calculated GPA, your LSAC-calculated GPA, all law schools previously attended, and more.

Since everything in this document is pretty much set in stone, the key things for you to know here is simply what this document contains so that you can know what may need more explanation from you in other parts of your application. There will likely also be questions in the actual law school application that schools can verify by looking at this sheet. That's worth noting because if you lie, withhold information, or provide inconsistent information in other parts of your application, the fact that the information contained here and elsewhere doesn't match will likely be a red flag for admissions officers. When such a red flag exists, there is a process for law schools to report inconsistencies and suspected dishonesty to LSAC, begin an investigation, and possibly reprimand you if there is sufficient evidence to suggest that you fudged part of your application. For example, questions about previous academic discipline, previously attending law school somewhere, and LSAT scores are likely to appear in your actual law school application. Thus, when the time comes later in your application to disclose or discuss these sorts of things, err on the side of honesty and disclosure.

Next, there are a number of things that law schools are likely to make note of off the bat when looking at this sheet. Things like your college major, LSAC-calculated GPA, LSAT scores, and any academic sanctions. Related to those things, here are a few tips and tricks to help you out when submitting your application packet:

1. You can apply and get in to law school with any major. However, if your undergraduate major was a STEM major, your undergraduate GPA is likely lower than that of someone without a STEM background. As discussed more in a later chapter, you are likely going to want to write a short and sweet GPA addendum highlighting that fact.

2. If you changed majors, schools are not going to know that unless you tell them. This sheet only shows your current

11

major (if still in school) or the major you graduated with. Thus, if you experienced an upward trend in grades or any other benefits by changing your major, you may need to write a GPA addendum explaining that as well.

3. When you LSAT score is listed, so is your "LSAT band". Admissions officers are taught to interpret this as meaning that despite your actual LSAT score, you could have easily scored anywhere within that band – with the lowest number being the lowest score you could have achieved and the highest number being the highest score you could have achieved. If you have taken the LSAT more than once, if your highest score falls outside of the band for your lowest score (typically if your highest score is 4 or more points higher than you lowest score) then it will most likely benefit you to write a LSAT addendum. More information about writing those can be found later in this book.

4. It's okay to take the LSAT multiple times. It's *common* in fact. Thus, unless you have something useful that you need to share about taking the exam multiple times (e.g., you were sick the first two times, you were consistently scoring higher on practice tests and wanted to achieve the same level of success on the actual exam, you took the exam three times before being diagnosed with a learning ailment that you later had the tools to deal with, etc.) there usually is not a need to write an addendum simply about

the number of times you have taken the test unless a school specifically asks you to. The assumption is usually that applicants retake the test because they want a better score.

5. If you take the LSAT more than four times then there is a chance that some schools will average your score. For four or less test attempts its most likely that schools will just take into account / place the most weight on your *highest* score. Granted, placing the most emphasis on the highest score is the admissions industry's norm *yet there are exceptions* / some schools that average multiple scores as a matter of policy irrespective of other factors. So be careful and always adequately study and prepare for the exam so that you can aim to try to get the best score possible the *first* time you take the exam.

6. Know that your LSAC-calculated GPA can be lower than your school calculated GPA. Because the LSAC-calculated GPA is the one that impacts law school rankings, that is the one that matters the most to admissions committees.

7. Related to point six, know that your LSAC-calculated GPA from your time in undergrad is the GPA that matters the most to law schools. Although any graduate degrees that you have are going to be listed on this sheet, they are more of a "resume enhancer" than anything else. Your

graduate GPA typically will not be used to offset a low undergraduate GPA. If that was your hope, later in this book I'll share other tips and tricks for possibly offsetting or helping a less than ideal GPA be seen as less of a blemish on your file.

The CAS Report: Transcripts

As is the case with your law school summary, by the time that you apply to law school your transcripts likely are what they are. Because you can't go back and modify your grades, do better in classes, etc., the best that you can do when it comes to your law school application is simply educate yourself on how your transcripts are likely to be reviewed and prepare to provide any useful context that may help an admissions committee look more favorably on your academic performance over the years. Since an upcoming section goes into more depth about GPA and other addenda, this chapter will simply focus on sharing some of the things that admissions officers are likely to look for and make note of when reviewing your transcripts.

First, any review of your transcripts is likely to begin with a cursory scan of your grades. How did you do in school in general? Mostly As? A few Fs and Ds? Lots of withdrawals? Too many pass/fail classes? Any semesters that seemed particularly off / where your grades were not as good as usual? These are all things that law school admissions committees are likely to take note of. Thus, if you have poor grades (Ds or Fs), lots of withdrawals, lots of pass / fail courses, or inconsistent grades across different semesters, then you may be someone who is going to want to write a GPA addendum when working on your application materials.

Next, admissions officers are likely to evaluate the level of rigor of the courses that you took. For example, as you moved beyond your freshman year did you begin to take more advanced courses? Or did you make the same mistake as I once did and fill your senior year's schedule with the easiest classes you could find (Jogging 101, Beginner Aerobics, Intro to Basket Weaving, etc.)? Just know that if you did the latter, that may hurt you slightly. Namely, that may cause an admissions committee to assume that your GPA is slightly inflated because you took seemingly easy classes as your college career progressed rather than challenging yourself with more rigorous courses.

The CAS Report: Writing Sample

As part of the LSAT, you must complete a written component of the exam. This writing sample is used by law schools to gauge both your writing and analytical skills. The key thing to know about the writing sample beforehand is that *there is* a right and a wrong way to complete it. Do not make the mistake of assuming that no one is going to read these or that completing it is just a formality. So much of being a good law student and good lawyer is tied to being a good writer, so these are often read very closely by admissions officers. In general, some of the smaller things that admissions officers are looking at includes your grammar, sentence structure, and ability to following elementary writing rules. With that in mind, there is sometimes a level of linguistic bias that admissions officers may have when reading these essays. Because a lot of my clients are from backgrounds in which English is not their first language, I want to highlight that disadvantage that many applicants of color may have when it comes to this timed writing sample. If that is in fact the case for you as well, you may benefit from explaining somewhere in your application materials that English is not your first language and that it takes a little longer for you to translate and write than it may take your counterparts.

Next, admissions officers are going to look at the substance of what you have written. This is what an admissions committee is going to place the most weight on, so if you are someone that may not be a strong writer under timed conditions because of the reasons discussed in the last paragraph, definitely try to make up for that by ensuring that the substance of what you write is great.

When it comes to answering a LSAT prompt properly, there are a few key things to know. First, there technically is no right or wrong choice. In reality, you simply need to be able to: (1) choose a side; (2) make a logical argument in support of that choice; and (3) present counterarguments in support of the other decision. If you've done those three things then you have done the writing sample correctly. Worth noting is that the thing that many applicants fail to do is number three: present counterarguments. Appendix B contains both a sample LSAT essay prompt and a sample answer to such. Worth noting is that the sample answer

16

I've written is likely a little too short – your answer should likely take up at least three full paragraphs which will likely take up at least (or very close to) one full page. In my experience, admissions officers rarely make note of what you argued, but they do make note of whether your arguments were sufficient, whether you provided counterarguments, whether your writing was good, whether your writing was short, etc. Knowing these things should help you put together a good writing sample when the time comes.

The CAS Report: Letters of Recommendation

In my first book, I talk about the difference between hard and soft factors. Worth noting however is the fact that I believe that although hard factors largely determine an admissions decision, they are by no means dispositive of whether you will be admitted to a school or not. In fact, I would estimate that hard factors typically make up about 60-70% of an admissions decision. While that it huge, the remaining 30-40% of an admissions decision is dependent on soft factors, and one-third (30%) to two-fifths (40%) of an admissions decision is by no means insignificant! With soft factors influencing that much of a decision, they often are what makes the difference between being waitlisted or admitted, denied or waitlisted, admitted with a measly scholarship package or admitted with a stellar scholarship package.

When it comes to soft factors, I am of the belief that your letters of recommendation are the most important part of your application package outside of your LSAT score and GPA. Thus, they are the most important element of your suite of soft factors. I say this because unlike other parts of your application, letters of recommendation are submitted by someone other than you and thus can appear to be some of the most objective and unbiased pieces of your application packet. Granted, letters of recommendation are often written by people who know you and are invested in your success in some way so there may be *a little* bias, but overall, it is assumed that recommenders have no incentive to be dishonest about how they feel about you. Especially since most applicants waive their right (which I recommend) to review their letters of recommendation once they have been uploaded to LSAC.

Because of the weight that this piece of your application materials can hold, it is to your advantage to know various ways that you can ensure that your letters of recommendation are as great as possible. Here are a few tips to ensure that:

Tip #1: Schedule a meeting. Before asking someone to write a letter of recommendation for you, ask to meet with them to chat. A virtual or in-person coffee meeting, visiting a professor during office hours, setting a meeting with your boss, or something similar is what I have in mind. During this meeting be prepared to do a temperature check on your potential recommender to try to get a sense of the things that they may say about you in a letter of recommendation. To prepare for this meeting, try to give some thought ahead of time to the types of things that you would like them to include in your recommendation letter. For example, if this is a professor, what can they say about your performance in class, how engaged you were as a student, the quality of your work, your analytical skills, how well you got along with other classmates, your performance on tests, etc. And what would you like them to say about these things? The same goes for an employer. What can they say about your work performance, your ability to be a team player, your analytical skills, how driven and thoughtful you are, the quality of your work product, etc.?

In your conversation with your recommender, consider opening the conversation by telling your recommender that you are hoping to go to law school and would like to know if they would be willing to serve as a recommender for you. From there, ask them what sorts of things they think they may write about. As they answer, feel encouraged to also offer some suggestions or your list of things that you would love for them to try to include. While you often can't control whether they actually include your list of items, by mentioning your items you only increase the likelihood that they will be included in your recommender's letter. As you continue your conversation, be sure to let your potential recommender know what your timeline is. Share where you are currently on your admissions journey, what you have left to do before finalizing your applications, what you have done already, and when you would like them to have their letter to you. Also ask your recommender if they need anything from you and share with them the things that you are able to share with them if it might be useful as they work on your letter (e.g., your personal statement draft, a resume, etc.). Also be sure to offer to send them a written list of the things that they already brainstormed with you regarding what they are thinking about including in their letter and possibly also a written copy of your list of the things that you would like for them to include. Appendix C contains a list of things worth having them discuss if they can.

Tip #2: Find out your rank. While having your meeting with your potential recommender, work in a way to ask them what numerical value they would give you if they had to assign a number to you. Specifically, if they had to compare you to your counterparts (other students, other employees, etc.) what would they rank you? If they say anything like "top 10%", "top 5%", "top 1%", "one of the best students ever", "one of the top 10 students in all their years of teaching", etc. then ask them to also include that in your letter of recommendation. If on the other hand they say something a bit more lukewarm (e.g., "top 50%", "top 25%", "average", etc.) then simply thank them for sharing and don't mention anything about including that in your letter of recommendation.

To the extent that your rank is good, having that included in your letter of recommendation is a great way to help you stand out to an admissions committee. Because the majority of letters of recommendation submitted for candidates tend to be relatively good, a good letter can easily become "average" since nearly everyone is saying positive things about whatever candidate they are writing about. One of the easiest ways for a letter of recommendation to be considered next level or above average is by including some sort of numerical comparison like this. For example, a letter that says that Nicole is a good student just doesn't hit as hard as a letter that says Nicole "is one of the top 5 students I've had in my 10 years of teaching." Thus, if you're able to get someone to say that you're ranked really high in comparison to others that they have taught or supervised, definitely ask them to include that in your letter.

This is a really important tip. When I worked in admissions, we literally had a system for rating letters of recommendation. Letters with red flags in them received a low number / score whereas letters with the highest number / score assigned to them almost always had to have some sort of numerical comparison like this in them.

Tip #3: Send a follow-up email and calendar invite. After you meet with your potential recommender, be sure to send them a follow-up email thanking them for their time, providing them with the materials you said you would (i.e., personal statement draft, resume, old paper, etc.), providing them with your notes / summary of the things you all discussed having them include in your letter, a sentence letting them know when (or that you already did) you will send the LSAC link for them to use to upload their letter, a sentence both reminding them of the deadline you all agreed to and telling them that you will (or have) sent them a calendar invite so that they can remember that deadline, and a sentence letting them know if / when you will follow-up with them. Then, if you haven't already, remember to send them that calendar invite with a reminder set for 3 days before the deadline so that they have on their calendar their promise to write your letter.

Tip #4: ALWAYS take "No" for an answer. Part of the reason for meeting with the potential recommender ahead of time is to get a sense of what they will say and of whether they are going to be a good recommender for you. If they seem lukewarm and unexcited when speaking *to you*, then that too is likely how they are going to come off when speaking *of you* in their letter of recommendation. The best recommenders tend to be people that are genuinely happy and excited for you, invested in your success / seeing you do well, and people that know you well enough to say something substantive about you.

If at any point a potential recommender seems hesitate or tries to politely decline your request to write a letter for you, let them. One of the things that frustrated me royally when I worked in admissions was reading either a bad or a half-hearted letter of recommendation. When I say a bad letter of recommendation, I mean just that – a letter in which the recommender said negative things about the candidate. It happens. And when I say half-hearted, I am thinking of the times when I read 2-3 sentence recommendation letters and thought "wow, they didn't even bother to at least cut and paste a letter or template from Google."

No matter how frustrated I would be with recommenders for writing poor letters, I also acknowledge that it's possible that these recommenders may've attempted to offer prior (perhaps verbal, perhaps nonverbal) cues that could have suggested to an applicant not to use them as one of their recommenders. Such cues were likely ignored or overlooked though. Thus, if you witness or think you're receiving any cues like this, go with someone else for your letter. Even if you notice the cues late / after already receiving the letter, consider not submitting it to law schools. Only submit letters that you think are likely to be good. See Appendix D for some LOR samples.

The EAPP

Now that we're done talking about the CAS Report, let's move on to the second file of documents that a law school will receive on your behalf. The EAPP (which stands for Electronic Application) contains your law school application, your personal statement, your resume, your addenda, and any other optional or supplemental essays or materials that you may submit to a school. Unlike the case with the CAS Report however, with the EAPP you have a lot of (if not sole) influence over how everything that a school receives with this file will look. Thus, you can really find ways to meaningfully stand out in a good way when it comes to your EAPP materials. This section will go into more detail explaining how.

The EAPP: Application

The actual application portion of your law school packet can be a mixed bag. In some instances, it can be pretty easy and straightforward to complete, yet in other instances it can be quite tedious. The key thing to know about this particular component of your application packet is that no matter how tedious it may feel, *do not rush through completing this.*

Oftentimes the application itself is composed of a mixture of "required" questions and "optional" questions. I cannot stress enough the importance of taking the time to answer every possible optional question, even if it means taking a break from completing the application to try to determine what the answer is or what you will say in response.

For first generation, low income, and minority applicants, it can be particularly important to answer questions about your parents, household, and economic background. Questions that try to elicit things like what your parents' highest level of education was, what their profession and income is, whether you grew up in a single-parent home, etc. As it is becoming increasing unpopular and litigious (if not illegal in some states) to give applicants an advantage due to their status as an underrepresented racial minority, more and more schools are looking at socioeconomic background as an alternative determinant for admitting a diverse cohort of students. Thus, while it often can feel like a source of shame or embarrassment to come from a background where you were nowhere close to being fed with a silver spoon, for admissions purposes, disclosing that reality can possibly enhance your chances of being admitted to a school.

Other optional questions that you might come across that you should make a point to answer include questions about any programs that a school has that you're interested in, questions about what other schools you're applying to, and questions about your academic or standardized test performance. To the extent that you are able to provide a school more information about yourself (e.g., what programs do we have that you're interested in, what led you to apply to our school, etc.) or more context about blemishes on your application (e.g., is there anything you want us to know about your LSAT score or GPA), you should definitely take advantage of the opportunity to answer.

The EAPP: Personal Statement

Law schools lie. Or stated more accurately, for some reason, law schools are notorious for having an overly broad or vague personal statement prompt that fails to give adequate direction regarding what you should *really* include in your personal statement. For example, here is a personal statement prompt that made me roll my eyes once upon a time:

> "The personal statement serves a number of purposes; unlike the LSAT writing sample, it gives the Admissions Committee the chance to evaluate your writing when you are not under pressure. It also gives the committee a chance to find out more about you personally. We strive

to have a diverse student body in terms of culture, interests, work experiences, etc. The personal statement gives you the opportunity to introduce yourself and elaborate on the diversity you are able to add to our entering class. The statement should describe any unusual aspects of your background that might provide an element of diversity in the law school. You should describe any skills or traits that you have had an opportunity to develop to an unusual level. Discuss as well any significant activities or work experiences that might enrich your law study."

I don't know about you, but from reading this prompt, I honestly wouldn't know what to write about. That's why I often tell my clients that a personal hill that I am willing to die on has to do with personal statements and the need to usually ignore what law school prompts say your personals statement should be about.

I am a strong believer that a good personal statement essentially focuses on two things: First, what is leading you to want to go to law school? What has served as a catalyst for your desire to become an attorney? Then, after you've discussed that, close out with a paragraph (or at least a sentence) that shares how you envision your future legal career. One of my favorite law school personal statement prompts basically expresses this sentiment this way:

"Your personal statement should be written in your own words and limited to 2-3 pages on a topic of your choice that will provide additional insight into your qualifications and interests. While there is no required topic, **if you are unsure of a topic, you may consider sharing why you are interested in pursuing a law degree and/or what your anticipated career goals/interests are at this time**."

Granted, I tend to require my clients to condense their personal statement down to two pages (with just a few, rare exceptions), but elsewise, the personal statement prompt above does a great job at succinctly guiding applicants in the right direction regarding what to write their personal statement about.

Think of your personal statement as your cover letter for law school. Only, instead of explaining what skills and traits you have that will make you a good law student, focus on what has motivated you to want to become a lawyer. What event(s) from your past served as a moment that sparked or crystallized your decision to want to be an attorney? What keeps you up at night or disturbs your spirit regarding the way our society functions? What issues are you passionate about and why – what sparked that passion? Although I have a great e-course entitled "Personal Statement Workshop" that you can find on my website (www.andersonadmissions.com) that focuses more on personal statements and how to write a good one, below are some general tips that I recommend you follow when putting together your law school personal statement:

1. Regardless of how many pages a school will accept, try to keep your personal statement down to two

pages. There are a few exceptions to this rule however, including the following:

a. If you're applying to a school that strongly encourages applicants to take advantage of all the pages you are allowed to submit (I believe Berkeley Law falls within this category) then feel free to write more.

b. If you're applying to a law school that explicitly instructs you to explain in your personal statement why you want to go to that specific law school, then write a two page personal statement and add your "why" explanation to the end of that – try to keep your essay to three pages though in this instance.

2. Always use standard margins and font no less than 11 pt. In some instances, schools may explicitly state that they want you to use 12pt or follow some other formatting rules – make sure you abide by those. Worth noting, I also personally prefer for applicants to use Time New Roman font as well.

3. Make sure your essay is double-spaced.

4. Always include a header on your personal statement that includes your name and the type of essay you are submitting (in this instance "personal statement) – this rule applies for every essay / supplemental material

that you submit. When you submit your materials, schools receive everything as one continuous PDF and unless you indicate which essay is which it can sometimes get hard to tell where one essay ends and another begins or which essay is being read at any given moment. You can also include your LSAC number in your header as some schools explicitly ask for that.

5. Don't worry about using page numbers / numbering your pages for your essays.

6. Don't make the mistake of "titling" your essay. You don't need a title. Personal statement is sufficient.

7. Avoid naming a law school in your personal statement unless the personal statement prompt explicitly asks you to explain why you want to go to that specific law school. If you are expected to explain this, then follow the same instructions provided below regarding writing a good "Why XYZ School" essay to see what sorts of things you need to include in this why explanation section of your personal statement.

8. Limit your personal statement to one or two stories / memories. When writing your personal statement, you want to be as focused as possible and try not to throw too much information at an admissions committee.

9. Towards the end of your personal statement, explicitly state what your current vision for yourself as a future lawyer is. Something short and sweet is fine, but the key is to state what kind of law you're currently interested in or what kind of clients you hope to someday serve. (E.g., "As a future civil rights attorney, I hope to someday help ensure that members of marginalized communities have quality legal representation.")

10. Avoid the urge to try to come up with a "catchy" opening. Just jump right into your story. Usually, seemingly "catchy" openings don't land well. Also, admissions officers have so many applications to read that "catchy" openings often just feel like fluff. It's much better to just get to the point / jump into the meat of what it is that you have to say.

11. Don't write about things unrelated to the answer to the questions of "what is motivating you to want to go to law school?" or "What made you decide that you wanted to be a lawyer?"

12. Avoid vulgar, overly familiar / casual, and cliché phrases. For example, instead of saying "I was pissed off as a result of…" say "I was enraged…"; instead of "That situation lived rent free in my mind" say "I couldn't stop thinking about that moment"; and

instead of saying "I want to be a voice for the voiceless" say "I am passionate about ensuring that members of xyz community have an opportunity to have their voice represented by a lawyer that understands them."

13. Don't regurgitate your resume in your personal statement.

See Appendix E for examples of personal statements that follow this model.

The EAPP: Diversity Statement

Diversity statements are often optional. Nevertheless, there tends to be a lot of confusion about who can or should submit one. The name "diversity statement" can be a bit of a misnomer in the sense that it leads many people to believe that to be eligible to write one, an applicant must have some form of diversity related to racial, ethnic, sexual, or gender identity. The truth however is that while those are things that you can write a diversity statement about, the best diversity statements tend to be more of a "challenges statement" that discusses how an applicant has overcome significant obstacles in life, such as socio-economic disadvantage, disability, being the first in their family to attend college, attending under-resourced schools, or other major hardships or challenges. Other challenges and hardships such as homelessness, working multiple jobs or long hours in high school or college, being undocumented, living in foster care, receiving government assistance, and subsisting at or near the federal poverty line are also examples of the types of disadvantages that tend to make great diversity statements.

Unlike the personal statement that ought to be pretty narrowly tailored and focused on explaining why you want to go to law school and what your post law school goals are, your diversity statement can be a bit more seemingly "all over the place." Stated differently, I often tell my clients that their diversity statement can be more of a "mini-autobiography". That means that its perfectly okay to share a narrative of your childhood, your teenage years, your college years, etc. in chronological order if you would like – picking and choosing the moments in your life's history that you want a reader to be aware of.

Oftentimes, the challenges that my clients have when it comes to writing their diversity statement are as follows: (1) not knowing what to write about; (2) ensuring that their diversity statement isn't redundant when placed next to their personal statement; and (3) feeling confused about which essay to use as their diversity statement versus their personal statement since the two can sometimes be interchangeable. Here's my advice for each of those concerns:

(1) think about the things that you have experienced in life that required you to demonstrate perseverance, resiliency, faith, hope, and fight / push through less-than-ideal circumstances. Those hard stories that require you to be vulnerable in order to share with others are often the most powerful.

(2) Know that it's okay if your personal statement and diversity statement *touch* on some of the same things. The

key thing, however, is that your diversity statement often is a place to expound upon something that you mentioned in passing in your personal statement. For example, I have a client that shared in passing in her personal statement that growing up in a household where drug addiction was present led to her desire to be a lawyer and how ultimately, she wants to be the kind of lawyer that helps to ensure that drug dependency is treated as a public health issue rather than criminalized. In her diversity statement however, she went into more depth and detail about what it was like growing up in such a household.

(3) The key difference between the personal and diversity statement is that the personal statement is about things that led to your desire to become an attorney. Sometimes my clients have experienced hardships that are worth sharing (e.g., growing up in poverty) that are unrelated to their professional aspirations (e.g., being an entertainment attorney). Thus, one way to figure out which essay to use for which is to think about which one answers the question of why you want to be a lawyer and making sure that that is your personal statement. In instances where both essays answer that question, then you likely want to use the one that is the most focused and the most powerful as your personal statement. The reason that I suggest using the most powerful one as your personal statement is multifold. First, your personal statement is often read first so you want that to be your strongest material (if possible). Second, not all schools will accept a diversity statement, so you definitely want your most powerful essay to be the one that you present to every school.

See Appendix F for examples of good diversity statements submitted alongside of personal statements.

The EAPP: Resume

Oftentimes, resumes are one area in which underrepresented applicants *truly shine* in comparison to their counterparts. The key to a good law school resume is simple: include *everything* that you have done outside of the classroom since being in college. Another unpopular opinion that I have regarding resumes is that if you are someone that also had to work while in high school (which is often the case for underrepresented applicants) then also consider including that as well. Ultimately, you want an admissions committee to review your resume and be able to determine a few things: (1) your time management skills, (2) your interests and commitments outside of a classroom, (3) your work ethic / ability to work hard or hustle, (4) your ability to maintain a job and employability post-law school. Don't make the mistake of thinking that your law school resume needs to only focus on things seemingly related to the practice of law.

Oftentimes applicants wonder how exactly they should format their resume, and the truth is that there is no specific right way. Things that I recommend however are the following:

(1) Know that it's okay to submit a two-page resume. Unless a school explicitly asks you to limit your resume to one page, do not delete anything from your resume to try to condense everything down to one page.

(2) Your resume should list your education, work experience, volunteer experience, hours worked / volunteered per week or per month, publications, leadership roles, and

possibly honors and awards. It's often okay to also include unpaid experiences on your resume (e.g, babysitting or serving as a caregiver for family members).

(3) Skills sections are often not necessary and something that I usually always advise my clients to delete. More often than not, they fail to add any probative value and just take up unnecessary space. If you have a skills section and are looking for something to cut to condense your resume any, start with this section. The one exception to this rule tends to be if your skills section is limited to *language* skills. Sharing with an admissions committee that you are fluent or proficient in another language is sometimes useful; but sharing on your resume that you are a team player, good at multitasking, proficient in Microsoft Word, etc. usually is not worth sharing.

(4) I know I stated this above kind of; but try to include with each work experience and especially with each volunteer experience how many hours per week or per month that you committed to that activity. If it varied, share what your commitment was on average or per season, for example: *Legal Intern (20 hrs / week)* or *Legal Intern (20 hrs / week during school year, 40 hrs / week during summers)*.

(5) If you are short on space, try to limit the number of bullets under each position to two or three. Instead of deleting roles or jobs that you have had, instead delete some of the descriptions / tasks that you provide regarding each.

(6) If you include a publications section and your past articles (or other things that you have written) can be found online, consider including a hyperlink for them when you reference them on your resume.

See Appendix G for an example of a good law school resume format. I like this sample because it does a great job of hitting on all the different sections that I think a good law school resume should contain. Of course, it's perfectly fine if you don't have some of these because they don't apply to you. Also, one section that's missing from this that you can add if applicable is a "Publications / Writings" section if you've published any papers, op-eds, etc.

The EAPP: Why XYZ School Essay

I stated earlier that I *strongly* advise my clients to *never* mention a law school by name in their personal statements unless a law school explicitly asks them to state in their personal statement why they want to attend that law school. The reason that I am so adamant about this is multifold:

(1) You don't need to name a law school in order to be admitted, in fact, most applicants that are admitted don't.

(2) When I worked in admissions I remember being on the receiving end of an application where all signs indicated that I was going to recommend a candidate for admission *until* I got to their personal statement and was hit with a sentence about how they wanted to attend *another* law school! Obviously, when this happened, it was clear that the applicant had simply failed to submit the right essay

or change out the name of the school to match the application, but such a mistake was (and can be for you) *fatal.* What was initially a strong file, likely to be recommended for admission, immediately became a file where the recommendation was "waitlist". While that may seem like a minor error with too steep of a consequence, for perspective, we received nearly 7,000 applications a year and only had 300 or so seats to fill. Personal statements are one of the main ways to weed out candidates (hence why I also believe schools are intentionally vague or overly broad with their personal statement prompt – to see who has enough intuition to write about the right thing *eye roll*) so tiny mistakes like this can truly be very detrimental.

(3) Because you have limited space when it comes to your personal statement (see my two-page rule above) you usually don't have enough room to provide a *substantive* explanation about why you want to go to a specific law school in your personal statement anyways.

(4) As an extension to my last point, more often than not, when applicants state a school's name in their personal statement, it is in a very shallow way and clear that they could have easily swapped the school's name out with another school's name and submitted the same essay to others. Because of this, these statements usually feel insincere.

Because of each of these things, I always advise my clients to write a *separate* "Why XYZ School" essay in lieu of mentioning a school in their personal statement *if* there is really something substantive that they want to share with an admissions committee about why they want to go there.

Worth noting, it is *perfectly okay* to neither mention a law school in your personal statement nor write a Why XYZ School essay. Most applicants admitted to law school each year do neither – so you can possibly fall within that category as well. At the same time however, there can be a slight advantage that you gain by writing an essay like this. Namely, because most applicants don't do something like this, it can help suggest that because you took the time out to do it that you are *really* interested in and serious about attending a specific law school. This can be useful in the sense of a school possibly being more willing to offer you a seat over a similar applicant because they feel more confident that you will positively impact their "yield" number which essentially tracks how many applicants that were offered a seat in the incoming class actually accepted it. Also, I know of some admissions committee members that simply like / enjoy these essays in general – it can feel heartwarming or endearing to some people, as if their school is truly special to you since you took the time out to present this extra information.

Should you decide to write a Why XYZ School essay, I tend to be of the belief that short and sweet is most ideal. This essay definitely should not be more than two-pages (double-spaced and following the same formatting rules I stated earlier for your personal statement). In fact, I recommend trying to stick to one-page if possible. I have even read some pretty good Why Essays that were as short as one paragraph. In fact, I know of at least one school that requires their Why Statements to be less than 400 words in length.

Regardless of whether you take my advice of writing a separate why statement or try to mention a law school in your personal statement, the key to writing a statement that stands out is simple: demonstrate that you *actually* did your homework on the school. The best way to do this is by focusing on the unique *academic* opportunities offered at whatever school you're writing to. When I'm talking to my clients, I package this advice this way: be sure to start your essay / lead it by naming 1-2 *specific classes* and 1-2 *specific professors* that you are interested in. From there, feel free to talk about clinics, student organizations, journals, geography, school culture, etc. that attract you to the school. Most applicants that write Why Essays however, tend to completely fail to talk about the actual unique academic opportunities (i.e., classes and professors) available at a school, and because of that, actually doing such can easily make you stand out.

See Appendix H for examples of good Why XYZ School Essays.

Addenda

Oftentimes applicants make the mistake of failing to write addenda when they really should. Writing an addendum to explain your grades / GPA, or LSAT performance can often benefit underrepresented applicants. However, too often applicants feel as if they are "making excuses" when they write these. In contrast, law school admission committees rarely read addenda and think that you are making excuses – rather, these are often seen as providing *useful context* that a school elsewise would not have had.

Also, if you have any character and fitness ("C&F") disclosures to make, writing a C&F addendum is likely going to be mandatory. Below I discuss some key things to know to help you when drafting any of these addenda.

Addenda: GPA / Grade Explanations

I tend to recommend that my clients submit a GPA or grade explanation addendum *anytime* that they believe that their GPA is less than what they believe that it could have been absent external circumstances, or anytime that there is useful context that they can provide about poor grades, rough semesters, etc. For underrepresented applicants, there are often a number of things that may negatively impact an applicant's undergraduate GPA, here are a few:

(1) Being first-generation and not understanding how to be a good student your first few years of college because you lacked guidance or failed to seek help.

(2) Having to work throughout school to finance your academics or support yourself financially.

(3) Having to support your family financially or by caring for siblings or other family members.

(4) Experiencing health issues.

(5) Having a (sometimes undiagnosed) learning or other ailment that you lacked the right tools to handle at the time.

(6) Experiencing a death or other tragedy (e.g., sexual assault, car accident, house fire, environmental disaster, etc.) in your family or life.

(7) Changing majors (especially if you went from a STEM major to something else).

Other times when you may also want to submit a GPA or grade explanation addendum include:

(1) Instances where you may want to explain what happened with *specific* grades, for example, if you withdrew from a lot of courses; failed, received a low grade in, or retook certain courses.

(2) If you had a semester or longer gap in your education.

(3) If you changed / transferred schools and experienced a change in academic performance (either positive or negative) as a result.

(4) If you had an upward trend in your grades and you want to call attention to that (e.g., perhaps you didn't take school seriously your first two years but had a complete turnaround by your junior and senior year).

(5) If you have been out of school for an extended period of time (this is particularly pertinent for nontraditional applicants) and you feel like your grades from years prior do not reflect the level of maturity and seriousness about your studies that you would now be able to commit to law school.

Again, as stated above it is important to know this: addenda are often viewed by admissions committees as *providing useful context* and not as *making excuses.* If you don't tell a law school what was going on with you at the time, then how are they going to know? Definitely take advantage of this opportunity to get your story regarding the circumstances surrounding your grades before an admissions committee so that they can use that information to your benefit / when making the case about (1) why you should be admitted or (2) how your past grades aren't an accurate reflection of your ability to succeed in law school.

As far as formatting goes and exactly how much you should say, I would say try to keep these addenda as short and sweet as possible. Only you know your story, but to the extent that you are able to condense it down to a paragraph great! Unless there was a lot going on, definitely try to keep it down to one page. Also, if you have both an academic and LSAT addendum, unless a school instructs you to do otherwise, put them on the same document but use bold and underlined section headers to distinguish between the two.

See Appendix I for examples of some good academic addenda.

Addenda: LSAT Explanations
As stated earlier, I always advise my clients to write an LSAT addendum if they have taken the LSAT more than once and their best score is four points or higher than their worst score. In essence, this explanation ought to explain what you attribute the change in your score to. A short and sweet explanation (3-4 sentences perhaps) often suffices here as well.

Beyond writing an LSAT addendum to explain that four-point or more increase in your score, I'm often on the fence about whether applicants should write one. Namely, I tend to find that most other

LSAT explanations wane in their level of persuasiveness. For example, oftentimes underrepresented applicants feel compelled to write addenda explaining that historically they have underperformed on standardized tests. In my experience however, addenda that express this are *only* persuasive or helpful if you're able to: (1) prove / show that your ACT or SAT score prior to college was not competitive yet (2) you were still able to maintain a *pretty high* undergraduate GPA. Unfortunately, however, oftentimes when applicants attempt to argue that they historically haven't done well on standardized tests they don't have the GPA to support the argument that they are still an extraordinary student despite past test performance. The reason that having that matters so much is because the admissions community has mixed feelings about this history of poor performance on standardized tests explanation. While some admissions professionals recognize that there are wide ranging problems (including serious racial as well as socioeconomic disparities) associated with using standardized tests as the measuring stick for law school performance, many other admissions officers are of the belief that law school and the bar exam simply replicate the standardized testing environment. Thus, those within that latter camp view it as a red flag when someone says that they simply aren't good at standardized tests, *especially* if that candidate lacks the ability to say "but, I still perform extremely well academically."

With all of this in mind, see Appendix J for examples of some good LSAT addenda.

Addenda: Character & Fitness Explanations
Unfortunately, when it comes to character and fitness issues (past academic discipline, past criminal history, etc.) there often is no

way to avoid having to write an addendum. Most schools have character and fitness questions such as those listed in Appendix K. If you answer in the affirmative to any of them then you usually *must* write an addendum to explain your answers.

The good thing about character and fitness disclosures however is that most things that applicants disclose (e.g., old speeding tickets, underage drinking, shoplifting as a thirteen-year-old, etc.) aren't serious enough offenses to hurt their chances of being admitted to law school. Typically, its more serious offenses however like sexual assault, DUIs, felony convictions, etc. that may cause an admissions committee to have pause or choose to interview you before deciding whether to grant you admission.

Some of my best pieces of advice when it comes to character and fitness addenda are as follows:

(1) **State the facts.** To the greatest extent possible share the 5 Ws (who, what, when, where, why) and the resolution. Who was involved? What happened? When did this happen? Where did it happen? Why did this happen? How was everything resolved?

(2) **Don't over disclose**. Keep in mind that different states have different character and fitness requirements so not all schools require you to disclose the same information. For example, in Alabama where I'm licensed, law school applicants may have to disclose any instances where they have ever been arrested. In California where I worked as an admissions officer however, applicants likely only have to disclose any instances where they have been convicted of a crime and not arrests that didn't result in a

conviction. Nevertheless, if an applicant submits their Alabama addendum which discloses an extensive arrest history to a California school, it could hurt their chances of admission despite the fact that they were never convicted of any of the things that they were arrested for. It's simply rarely a good idea to share negative information about yourself that you weren't asked to share. Oftentimes all that does is add blemishes to your file and make an admissions committee view you in a less positive light and question whether it would be wise to admit you. Moral of the story: pay close attention to each school's character and fitness questions and make sure that you're only disclosing what is asked of you.

(3) **Take accountability and discuss any lesson(s) learned from past mistakes**. As is the case with all the other addenda, this explanation does not need to be long and drawn out – short and sweet suffices. Simply make sure that after explaining the 5 Ws listed above that you also explain how you have grown / changed as a result of the experience.

(4) **Don't lie or provide misleading information.** While it may be uncomfortable having to relive or share stories that paint you in a less-than-ideal light, remember that everything that you disclose to a law school will be shared with the State Bar when it's time for you to graduate / apply to become an attorney. Thus, lying in this initial disclosure can often be worse than whatever your offense was and serve as something that precludes you from being able to practice law.

See Appendix L for examples of some good character and fitness addenda.

Chapter 2: Finding the Right School for You!

Historically, underrepresented applicants have not always fared as well as their counterparts when it comes to being admitted into law school. For example, it's no secret that the legal profession is not very diverse. In my first book I share statistics regarding the makeup of the legal profession in comparison to the makeup of the United States population. Not surprisingly, as the pipeline to the legal profession, law schools often reflect this jarring lack of diversity as well – within the student class, the faculty, the administration, etc. Simply across the board. Even more disheartening than the lack of diversity within law schools is the fact that nearly 50% of Black applicants are not accepted to a single law school and that only 5% of students at top law schools come from the bottom 25% of the socioeconomic stratosphere.

I could talk for days about many of the unfair barriers to entry that low-income, first generation, and minority applicants face, but instead, I'll devote this chapter to trying to assist you with being strategic with regard to the way that you approach choosing which schools to apply and commit to. In the next few pages, I will discuss some of the ways to enhance your chances of becoming a lawyer either at the school or your dreams or with a scholarship package that makes you smile.

Deciding on Where to Apply
It's my belief that of the reasons that underrepresented applicants don't always fare as well as their counterparts when it comes to being admitted to law school is that we don't always do the best job at applying to a healthy mix of different law schools. For example, it's not uncommon for underrepresented applicants to apply to *less* law schools than their counterparts. In addition, many times we also do not know how to put together a list of law schools to apply to that match our credentials. And finding

schools that match our credentials is much more complicated than simply applying to schools based on name recognition or where our numbers fall in relation to their medians. The next few pages will be devoted to providing advice designed to help you avoid making either of these two mistakes.

Shooting Your Shot the Right Number of Time – Applying to the Right Number of Law Schools

I once read that law school applicants saw a greater chance of being admitted to law school if they applied to at least ___ schools. Thus, I always advise my clients to aim to apply to about 8-10 different law schools. That's 3 "safety" schools, 3 "target" schools, 2 "reach" schools, and up to 2 more schools in any of those categories you choose. Granted, I know that applying to law school can get expensive, so even if money is a barrier, then I recommend aiming to apply to at least 5. With this approach, that's 2 "safety" schools, 2 "target" schools, and 1 "reach" school.

Again, I know that applying to law school can get pretty expensive, so if you haven't already, pick up my first book *Applying While Black (or Brown)* and check out the chapter devoting to discussing ways to offset application costs. In a nutshell, LSAC's Candidate Referral Service (CRS), LSAC's fee waiver application, LSAC Forums, and law school events are going to be some of your best resources for getting application fees waived.

Creating Your Law School List

Great. Now that you know how many law schools to apply to, how exactly should you go about putting together your law school list? Well here's where things get much more complicated. In a second, I'll share how to determine what is considered a "safety", "target", or "reach" school for you, but before then I'll share some things that you are going to want to ask yourself before you even get to that point. To help you figure out what law schools you may be interested in attending or considering, take the time to ask yourself the following questions:

(1) What are your geographic preferences? Would you prefer to attend law school:
    a. Near your support system?
    b. In the same area that you hope to practice law?
    c. Someplace warm or cold?
    d. In a big city or small town?
    e. In a specific region?
    f. With a specific cost or style of living (e.g., cost of rent, easily accessible public transportation, affordable apartments within a certain proximity to your school).

(2) What are your academic interests? Are there:
    a. Specific areas of law that you are interested in studying (e.g., intellectual property, entertainment law, environmental law, public interest, etc.) or specializations that you want a school to offer a certificate in?
    b. Specific kinds of learning environments you prefer (e.g., being taught by professors of color, having large or small class sizes, having a certain percentage of other underrepresented students in school alongside you, etc.)?
    c. Certain kinds of hands on / experiential learning opportunities (e.g., clinics, mock trial, externships, etc.) that you want to have access to?

(3) What are your post-law school career aspirations?

    a. How important is a law school's rank to you? Namely, do you need to go to a Top 14 or Top 50 law school because you want to start your legal career in any of the following areas:

        i. Big Law (or at a prestigious / large-sized law firm)?

        ii. a Federal Clerkship (working for a federal judge)?

    b. Do you know where you want to practice law at or are you open to ending up wherever?

    c. What are your starting salary goals and expectations?

    d. Would you prefer a career services office that essentially aids in summer clerkships and post-law school opportunities being handed to you, or are you okay with having to hustle harder to network and elsewise find opportunities on your own?

(4) How debt-adverse are you?

    a. How much does financing your legal education with as few loans as possible matter to you?

    b. Would you rather go to an expensive (meaning you'll have to take out a lot in student loans) law school that puts you in a better position to get a prestigious high-paying job right after law school or one that costs less (meaning you'll have to take out less in student loans) yet positions you to get a good job with a decent salary right after law school?

    c.   What is your personal student loan limit / cap – the number that you're comfortable with having to take out to finance your legal education?

While there are no right or wrong answers to any of these questions, the answers are going to be instrumental to helping you figure out what law schools to consider. Although the answers will be drastically different for each applicant, knowing them is going to play a significant role in helping you to create your list of 8-10 (or 5) schools once you've followed the steps in the next section to identify your safety, target, and dream schools.

Identifying Your Safety, Target, and Dream Schools

Okay, so I'm about to throw a number of different tools at you to help you determine your safety, target, and dream schools. Worth mentioning however, is that to come up with an accurate list you are going to need an LSAT score. If you haven't taken the LSAT yet, that's okay – for now you can play around with whatever your most frequent score on practice tests has been or with the score you received on your first diagnostic exam. If you are thinking about applying to law school you ought to have at least taken a diagnostic exam and should be devoting somewhere between six months to a year preparing for the actual exam via practice tests, studying, etc. for it. Thus, even if you haven't actually sat for the exam yet, you should have a guestimate of where your score may fall. Also, if you have multiple LSAT scores on file then use your highest score for these exercises.

7 Sage's Law School Predictor

Over a decade ago when I was applying to law school, I was able to put together my list of schools to apply to using a website: www.lawschoolpredictor.com. That tool essentially allowed me to plug in my LSAC-calculated GPA and LSAT score to see what my odds of admission (strong likelihood, weak likelihood, etc.) were at every law school in the country. Well, that website is no longer operational, but a similar website that I like a lot is 7 Sage's Law School Predictor (insert website link).

Similar to how LawSchoolPredictor.com once worked when I was applying to law school, with 7 Sage's law school predictor, you plug in your numbers, click the box that says "URM" if you're an underrepresented minority, select the month that you will be applying, and let the computer calculate your odds of being admitted to each school across the country. While any prediction tool look this is of course going to be imperfect, I do appreciate its utility, nonetheless.

I recommend using 7 Sage's Law School Predictor when determining your safety, target, and reach schools. Using this tool, I recommend considering a safety school any school where you have an 80-100% chance of being admitted, a target school any school where you have a 50-79% chance of being admitted, and a reach school any school where you have less than a 50% chance of being admitted.

The reason that I like 7 Sage's percentage-based calculator is because it mirrors the way admissions work actually looked for me. For example, when I worked in admissions, based on someone's GPA and LSAT score, I had internal data available that told me what percentage of applicants with those numbers were admitted last cycle. If someone's stats suggested that they had a 75% chance of being admitted last cycle, a 50% chance of being admitted last cycle, or a 10% chance of being admitted last cycle, then I reviewed their file as if they had the same odds of being admitted this cycle. That means that someone with a 75% chance was *more likely than not* to be admitted and that my review of their file would mostly require me to be on the lookout for any red flags or things that suggested they might not be a good fit at our school. A 50% chance meant that it was a coin toss / could go either way for that applicant and when reviewing their file I needed to determine whether they were someone that significantly impressed me (*suggesting I should recommend them to be admitted*) or if they were simply average or had too many red flags (with these latter two categories *suggesting I should recommend them to be waitlisted or rejected*). And a 10% chance meant that they were most likely to be denied yet there was a possibility that I would find somethings in their file that indicated that they were extremely impressive candidates despite their numbers and that if I wanted to recommend them for admission then I likely needed to have a strong case to justify why.

Anywho, once you plug in your numbers and see which schools fall within which of those three categories for you, feel free to create a long list of the schools that stand out to you initially based on things like ranking and geographical location. Then take that long list and spend some time researching each of the schools on your list to learn more about their unique curricular offerings, culture, etc. As you learn more about each school, start comparing what you're finding to the questions you answered earlier about what you're looking for in a school. As you cross-reference these two lists, you should be able to narrow your law school list down some. Other ways to research schools and help narrow your list down includes attending law school fairs or LSAC Forums and talking to admissions officers at them, attending virtual or in-person law school tours, attending law school open houses or other events designed for prospective law students, etc.

LSAC's Law School Profiles

As you research individual schools as I suggested in the last section, law schools' websites ought to be a great resource for you. Another good resource however is LSAC.org that provides law school profiles for just about every law school in the nation. I recommend that you check out the LSAC-hosted law school profiles of the schools you're interested in both to learn more about a school *and* to learn more about your chances of admission at particular schools. While 7 Sage's Law School Predictor may do a sufficient job at giving you a general idea of what your odds are at different schools, LSAC's law school profiles can sometimes help you glean more information about your odds of admissions at certain law schools. Specifically, if you scroll to the bottom of a law school profile, you're sometimes able to find an applicant profile similar to the one below, in Table 1.

What these profiles do is provide past data of applicants. Essentially, by using these grids, you can gain insight into what your odds of admission at a specific school might have been in a past cycle. And because law schools are often trying to duplicate the stats of the classes they previously brought in (in order to maintain their rank) this grid can definitely help provide insight into what your odds may be in the current cycle.

So how do you use these grids? First, know that the data provided is usually not from the current incoming class. It's more likely that the grid is for two admissions cycles ago / students that are currently 2Ls at a school. So if a law school happened to have had a significant change in rank over the last year (which occasionally yet rarely happens) then this grid may not be as useful. Because most schools however tend to maintain their rank year after year, knowing what the odds are of getting in two years ago is likely very helpful in determining what the odds are of getting in this cycle. Why do I think that? Because when I worked in admissions, my process of reviewing applications literally began with me taking a look at the candidate's stats (GPA / LSAT score) and comparing their numbers to those of students that got in last cycle.

Anywho, unlike 7 Sage's Law School Predictor where you plug in your numbers and get a percentage telling you your chances of being admitted to law school, here, you plug in your numbers (or find yourself within the chart) and find out how many people with similar numbers to you applied in a past cycle and how many got in. For example, with the grid listed below for UC Irvine, you can see that in a past application cycle (most likely 2020-2021) that 226 applicants applied with an LSAT score between 145-149 and 4 were admitted. Of those people that were admitted with an LSAT score within this range, 2 had a GPA over 3.75 and 2 had a GPA between 3.5-3.74. Given the fact that UCI's median LSAT score and GPA was a 163 and 3.57 in 2020, and their 25th percentile numbers were 161 and 3.4 that same year, this chart helps indicate some of my favorite points:

(1) *You do not have to have a school's median numbers in order to be admitted to law school.* Stated differently, don't reject yourself simply because your numbers don't fall within a school's median or 25th percentile range.

(2) *A median is simply the point that half of applicants fell above and below and a 25th percentile is often not the same as the lowest or cutoff number for a school.* In order to get a better sense of what's the *lowest* score that you

can have and still have a fighting (even if slim) chance of being admitted use these charts.

(3) *Most applicants admitted to law school are splitters.* If you are able to have *at least* one number – LSAT score or GPA that is at a school's median great, odds are that you have a fighting chance at being a competitive applicant even if your other number is significantly below the median or 25th percentile.

(4) *If you have a strong enough file, it is possible to be admitted to law school with both numbers below a school's median.* If you find yourself with both numbers below the median, aim to have at least one number (if not both) with the 25th percentile, but there is likely going to be a handful of applicants without that as well that is granted admission.

Table 1: The University of California Irvine's Applicant Profile, (taken from LSAC.org on January 2, 2022)

APPLICANT PROFILE

Using the Applicant Profile Grid

LSAT Score	3.75+ Apps	3.75+ Adm	3.50–3.74 Apps	3.50–3.74 Adm	3.25–3.49 Apps	3.25–3.49 Adm	3.00–3.24 Apps	3.00–3.24 Adm	2.75–2.99 Apps	2.75–2.99 Adm	2.50–2.74 Apps	2.50–2.74 Adm	2.25–2.49 Apps	2.25–2.49 Adm	2.00–2.24 Apps	2.00–2.24 Adm	Below 2.00 Apps	Below 2.00 Adm	No GPA Apps	No GPA Adm	Total Apps	Total Adm
170–180	14	13	11	8	11	10	6	3	9	5	4	1	0	0	0	0	0	0	4	4	59	44
165–169	59	53	88	76	46	39	29	19	20	7	6	2	2	0	0	0	0	0	7	5	257	201
160–164	139	84	200	106	157	53	95	12	37	1	12	0	5	1	2	0	0	0	35	11	682	268
155–159	95	25	158	25	141	6	67	3	30	2	21	0	3	0	5	0	1	0	24	0	545	61
150–154	58	7	99	2	77	3	60	1	41	1	17	0	10	0	4	0	1	0	13	0	380	14
145–149	21	2	40	2	48	0	43	0	31	0	16	0	15	0	1	0	2	0	9	0	226	4
140–144	10	1	17	0	18	0	18	0	25	0	13	0	6	0	2	0	1	0	10	0	120	1
Below 140	3	0	5	0	6	0	9	0	16	0	11	0	3	0	3	0	0	0	3	0	59	0
Total	399	185	618	219	504	111	327	38	209	16	100	3	44	1	17	0	5	0	105	20	2328	593

Apps = Number of Applicants
Adm = Number Admitted
Reflects 99% of the total applicant pool; highest LSAT data reported.

See Appendix M for visual instructions on how to find this and similar charts using LSAC.org.

A Final Note on Enhancing Your Odds of Being Liked by a Law School

So, what is it about someone with numbers below a law school's median or with low chances of being admitted that causes them to still be admitted? For most people it isn't simply luck. You likely have an extremely impressive and compelling narrative and package to be the candidate with lower credentials that gets into law school. For every applicant this looks different, but for some people this means things like having a heartbreaking yet also heartwarming story of overcoming hardships and tragedy; having an impressive professional background such as coming to law school after a decorated military, athletic, entertainment or other career; etc.

One easy thing that applicants can do to stand out (in addition to taking advantage of the opportunity to tell their story in a compelling way using the personal statement and diversity statement tips provided earlier) is to find a way to interact with an admissions officer. Obviously, you don't want to be too pushy or annoying, but something as simple as meeting and talking to an admissions officer at a LSAC Forum and following up with a simple "thank you email" is a really small yet sometimes impactful thing that candidates can do. You can also send another thank you email to the admissions officer you met with once you finally submit your application – simply letting them know that thanks to their talk with you your interest in their school was cemented and you have since submitted your application and look forward to receiving a decision in the coming weeks.

The reason that I like to recommend making personal contact is because for many schools this is the closest thing to an interview that you're able to get. In fact, some admissions officers actually treat meetings with prospective students like informal interviews whether the applicant knows it or not. When interacting with candidates, some admissions officers are paying close attention to the way you present yourself, interact, your interests, whether you seem to have a good head on your shoulders or an employable personality, etc. From there, they may also make notes of their impressions of you and eventually add these to your file. So, if you really hit it off with an admissions officer, all the more reason to follow up with a thank you email – so that they can add both that and their impressions of you to your file. For several candidates, this personal interaction is a game changer for them when it comes to the final admissions decision.

Also, for candidates with less competitive numbers, riding out the waitlist may be a really wise strategy to help them get into their dream or reach school. More on that in a coming section. ☺

Chapter 3: I've Applied – Now What?

After you've applied to law school, it can easily take an average of eight to ten weeks to hear back from schools. Granted, this applies to schools with *rolling admissions* specifically. While some applicants receive decisions much earlier than this, it's not necessarily a bad sign if it's been nearly two months and you still haven't received a decision yet. Keep in mind that different admissions officers read applications at different speeds and some members of admissions committees have one job: read files, while others have multiple jobs: read files, attend recruitment events, plan admitted student days, interview applicants, etc. If you find yourself waiting to hear back from schools and it has been more than ten weeks (make an exception for weeks with major holidays / school breaks such as Thanksgiving week and the last two weeks in December) then it is typically perfectly fine to reach out to a law school either via email or phone call to check on the status of your decision. See Appendix N for an example of what such an email could look like.

Final law school decisions are often going to be one of three things: admit, waitlist, or deny. In addition to these three decisions, some law schools may notify you that they have decided to *hold* your file until a certain date – while similar to a waitlist decision, this is not quite the same thing. Below I explain further what each decision means:

- Admit: Congratulations! You're in! An admittance is pretty self-explanatory. It means that the school has decided to offer you a seat in the upcoming class and that in order to reserve that seat you must follow whatever steps a school has set forth in your admissions letter – usually, place a seat deposit (or two) by a certain date. It is *imperative* that you actually pay attention to and follow whatever steps are listed in your acceptance offer to reserve your seat if you in fact want to go to that school. I have seen applicants who have made the mistake of *forgetting* to place their seat deposit at the school of their choice and subsequently (worst case scenario) ending up either losing their spot in the class and having to reapply, or (better case scenario) having to wait a year before being able to start law school.

- Waitlist: Being on the waitlist essentially means that the admissions committee saw something that they liked when reviewing your file yet at the same time your file may not have been the strongest. Nevertheless, the admissions committee wants to hold on to your file to make a determination at a later date about whether to admit you based on how the rest of the class shapes up or if space becomes available. When you're placed on the Waitlist you should likely send a letter of continued interest (LOCI) once a month beginning in late-April / early May expressing the fact that you are grateful for being on the waitlist and would welcome a seat in the upcoming class if one becomes available. Of course, this rule may change based on the schools you're waitlisted at – so feel free to reach out to individual schools to ask them how they would recommend you managing being on the waitlist and how frequently you should reach out. For many law schools, the waitlist is maintained throughout the summer before law school starts and someone can be pulled from it as late as the first week of orientation (if not the first week of school itself). Thus, if you remain interested in attending a law school even that close to the start of the semester, then definitely keep sending your LOCIs throughout the summer up until school starts or you receive a final decision (admit or deny).

- Hold: The main difference between being on "hold" and being on the "waitlist" is that being on hold typically means that a school will reevaluate your file *by a specific date* and make an admit, waitlist, or deny decision by then. For example, if a school tells you that they will hold your file until *February 29ᵗʰ* that is very different than being on the waitlist until the week that law school starts.

- Deny: Unfortunately, being denied is pretty self-explanatory as well. If you end up being rejected by a law school however, you are typically able to reach out to that law school *during the summer* to ask if you can chat with an admissions officer to find out what you could have done differently or improved in your application. This is a smart thing to do if you are open to waiting a year (or more) to start law school and reapplying in a later cycle. Some schools even have an appeal process where you can ask them to reconsider their denial – in fact, I recently had a client who went through such a process and had her denial for this cycle reversed / turned into an admittance after she wrote a letter to appeal her decision (she also had a new / higher LSAT score to justify why she was appealing the denial).

Negotiating Scholarships

While in some instances, scholarship offers are pretty much set in stone, in many instances they are not. An added benefit of applying to numerous (and a healthy mix) of schools as discussed earlier is the fact that getting into multiple schools with competing scholarship offers can oftentimes give you the ability to leverage different schools' scholarship offers against one another. In my experience, underrepresented students – especially low-income and minority applicants – are more hesitant to their counterparts to attempt to negotiate their scholarships, or at times don't even know that they can attempt to do such a thing. Since there is some level of strategy and best practices that I suggest when it comes to negotiating scholarships, if you find yourself in a position where you are curious about how to do such, I encourage you to visit my website (www.andersonadmissions.com) and purchase my e-course entitled 10 Tips on Negotiating Scholarships.

Deciding Where to Place a Seat Deposit

When deciding on where to place your seat deposit, your determination should not be made absent revisiting the assessment you made for yourself in Chapter 2 when choosing your school list. Based on the schools that you got into, which most closely align with the things that are most important to you? While for some students (i.e., those hoping to clerk for the Supreme Court, or become partner at the largest most prestigious law firm in the country, etc.) going to a top ranked law school is essential, for other students (i.e., those hoping to go into big law but with as little student loan debt as possible) going to a T50 law school may make more sense, whilst for other students (i.e., those willing to hustle to find their own job opportunities, those who want no student loan debt, or those with less success during the admissions process) going to a lower ranked school may make the most sense.

Unfortunately, there is no cookie-cutter answer for what school makes the most sense for each applicant. If you find yourself in a position where you are weighing your school options and need someone to go through the pros and cons of each option with you, I'd be more than happy to do that with you. Simply visit my website (www.andersonadmissions.com) and consider scheduling a 30- or 45-minute one-on-one Q&A Session / Zoom Call with me.

Navigating the Waitlist

When I worked in admissions, I had the honor of managing the waitlist for the school that I worked at. While every law school is going to be different, my advice on navigating the waitlist comes from my personal and unique experience of being the person responsible for rereviewing and organizing waitlist files, keeping up with letters of continued interest ("LOCIs") received, and creating short-lists or interviewing candidates, and making recommendations on who should be pulled from the waitlist. With that in mind, below are a few things that I recommend doing to help increase your odds of possibly being pulled from the waitlist at whichever school you hope to attend.

(1) **Send a letter of continued interest once a month** – or every 4 to 6 weeks – beginning as early as April (most schools don't even think about pulling students from the waitlist until after their first or second deposit deadline. Since the first deposit deadline for most schools is mid-April, lining up your first letter to arrive shortly before or after that deadline is wise).

    a. Think of your first LOCI as a "Why XYZ School" essay. Even if you already shared this in your initial application, reiterate why you want to go to

66

that specific school. Be sure to touch on the following things if you can:

    i. 1-2 professors that you want to take classes under

    ii. 1-2 elective (2L or 3L) course that you hope to take

    iii. 1-2 clinics, journals, student organizations, specializations, etc. that interest you

    iv. Brief mentions of past contacts you've had with the school (i.e., law school tours, attending an open house, talking with an admissions officer at a law school fair, meeting current students / alumni / professors, etc.)

    v. Any geographic ties you have to the area (or your reason for wanting to be in that area)

    vi. Any changes to your application file since you applied (i.e., new job, etc.)

b. Know that letters of continued interest don't have to be long. Especially not after your first in-depth one. Honestly, law schools understand that there's not much new you can say every month about why you want to go to their school. Thus, Appendix O provides a short and sweet LOCI template that you can use for any letters after your first one.

(2) Schedule a law school tour. Even absent an admission to a school, you can demonstrate your interest in attending the school by scheduling a law school tour or class visit (if the school allows either). Afterwards, you may even have an opportunity to meet an admissions officer (see next tip) as law school admissions officers sometimes have open office hours for prospective students either right before or right after scheduled tours and class visits.

(3) Meet with an admissions officer. While different schools have different protocol regarding who has access to or who can meet with admissions officers, generally speaking, it is not hard to get 5-15 minutes' worth of face time with an admissions officer if you visit the school in person (see tip above) or send an email requesting a short meeting (I recommend explicitly saying that you'd love to talk with someone for *only 5 to 15 minutes)*.

    a. Once you have your meeting be prepared for this to possibly be treated like an informal interview. As stated in a previous section, whether an admissions officer tells you or not, they will likely make mental notes during your conversation and add their impressions of you to your file after you all are done chatting. Thus, to put your best foot forward, here are a few things you should be prepared to discuss should you get your 5 to 15 minutes with an admissions officer:

        i. Be able to clearly and succinctly articulate why you want to go to law school (what has served as your catalyst), your vision for yourself post-law school, and why you want to go to that *specific* law school.

        ii. Be prepared to ask 2-3 questions about things that you can't easily find by doing a quick Google Search or checking out the school's website (e.g., "How many students do you anticipate pulling from the waitlist this year?"; "Is there anything that I should do to help enhance my odds of being pulled from the waitlist besides sending regular letters of continued interest?"; "How active is your Business Law Students Association"; "Where do students typically find housing in the area – does your office have any guides or resources to help admitted students find a place to live?"; etc.)

    iii. Be as respectful of the admissions officer's time as possible. It's pretty standard for someone to talk with a prospective student for 5 minutes, 15 minutes is usually close to the max, and 10 minutes is probably the sweet spot that you want to stay within.

    iv. Try to let your warmth or other positive personality traits shine through – even if in a nonverbal fashion.

(4) Stop sending LOCI once you no longer remain interested in attending the law school. Believe it or not, LOCI are most useful to schools in the sense that it allows them to easily tell which of the hundreds of applicants on their waitlist are the *most* interested in being pulled from the waitlist. While law schools may have priority, regular, and other waitlist categories, LOCI help a school know which candidates in any of those categories it may be wisest to invest the most time into (whether reevaluating their files first, calling them for interviews, etc.) as they are more likely to accept an offer of admission if they were to receive one. It's essentially an easy way for law

69

schools to create "short lists" of folks to seriously consider pulling from.

Granted, there are often other ways that schools also make shortlists of candidates to consider from the waitlist (i.e., high GPAs, high LSAT scores, interesting backgrounds, etc.), however even these lists are sometimes cross-referenced with the list of people that have sent a LOCI in recently. Because law schools often pull candidates from the waitlist as late as orientation or the first day of school, for many candidates, being pulled from the waitlist at some point becomes an unattractive possibility. For example, if you live in DC and want to be pulled from the waitlist for a school in California, you may not be willing to be accept an offer to attend if it comes the first week of school – especially not considering the logistical nightmare that it may be to find and secure housing as well as make a cross-country move at the drop of a hat. Thus, it makes sense to stop sending LOCI in June, or whenever that point of "I wouldn't go there at this point" arrives.

(5) Know that interviews are likely designed to assess your personality. Some schools interview candidates before pulling them from the waitlist. If you yourself are invited to do an in-person or Zoom interview, be prepared with the same information from Tip 3 above – know the answers to those questions, have a few questions prepared to ask, and let your positive personality traits shine. While every school has its own unique culture and thus may desire different character traits from applicants, I think that it's safe to say that these sorts of character traits don't go unnoticed (in a positive way): intellectual curiosity, the ability to hold an intelligent conversation, warmth and kindness, considerateness, a sense of humor, seeming like you are a team-player / can get along with and work well with others, having confidence (yet not arrogance), etc.

During your interview, you are likely to be asked a mixture of soft-ball questions (i.e., Why do you want to attend here? Why do you want to be a lawyer? Etc.) and questions that may be a bit harder to answer (i.e., What is a current event that you have strong opinions about currently? What is the last book you read and what was it about? What was your favorite class in undergrad and why – what was your favorite concept to learn? Etc.). While those questions in that latter category may require more thought or catch you off guard, know that there most likely truly is no right or wrong answer to the question. Again, admissions officers are likely really trying to figure out what your personality is like, how you answer / respond to questions (your confidence level, your ability to articulate your thoughts concisely, how you may be during an employment interview / your employability, etc.).

(6) Send updated materials if a school will allow it. This can include an updated resume (if you've gotten a new job), new transcripts (if you've graduated since being admitted), new letters of recommendation (should be sent directly from the recommender to the school if the school will allow it), etc.

(7) Don't be too pushy or persistent. I know that this may sound counterintuitive to many applicants reading this book. Especially since those of us from underrepresented and low-income backgrounds have gotten comfortable with "hustling" and working twice as hard to secure opportunities. However, it can feel overwhelming at times for admissions officers to be in constant contact with candidates. Do what you can to make a good impression using the suggestions above, but then be willing to step back and just wait (while doing nothing else besides sending that regular LOCI) to hear back from the school. You don't want to be too aggressive or appear to be desperate, so there is a tight line to toe when deciding how many additional contacts to have with each school.

Applying as a Transfer Applicant

Transferring law schools is a great way to obtain the benefits of being a graduate of a specific law school despite the fact that you did not complete your 1L year at said school. Worth noting however is that there are both pros and cons to transferring law schools:

Pros of Transferring

- Can move to a higher ranked, more prestigious, or other school that elsewise complements your geographic, programmatic, or other preferences
- Get to enjoy the benefits (e.g., employment outcomes / career services resources, prestige, etc.) of being a graduate of your new law school
- Can possibly end up at your dream school or a school that you really wanted to go to as a 1L but couldn't get into (e.g., was waitlisted or denied)
- Can expand your network of future lawyers / colleagues that you know

- Have access to new (possibly unique) opportunities such as participating in your new school's OCI; joining a journal; trying out to be on moot court or mock trial; possible access to unique clinics, specializations, or certificate programs; etc.

Cons of Transferring
- May have to give up a scholarship whilst being ineligible for one from your new school (many schools don't offer scholarships to transfer students)
- May have to work harder to build community (as you no longer have your 1L friends and weren't a part of any 1L small sections at your new school) or may miss your friends and professors from your first school
- You likely won't have a class rank so may have to get creative when demonstrating your competitiveness or credentials to prospective employers

Essentially to be a strong transfer applicant you want to do a few things. First, you want to do well as a 1L at your initial school. Second, you want to have a compelling explanation regarding why you believe the school you are applying to as a transfer student is a more ideal fit for you. That explanation should not discuss a school's rank or prestige, nor should it bad mouth your initial school. In addition, you may need to be able to demonstrate that you have built strong relationships with (and were liked by) professors at your 1L school. Also, you want to be able to demonstrate (via your resume or elsewise) that you will make a positive contribution / be an asset at your new school.

Lastly, you want to be someone who might have had a chance of being admitted (even a slim chance counts) as a 1L. The tools shared in Chapter 2 can help you determine that. For example, if you plug in your numbers using 7Sage's Law School Predictor and you use your numbers from before starting law school, click the URM box if applicable, and select the earliest application month possible, do you have at least a 1% chance of being admitted? Or, when looking at a school's applicant profile grid on LSAC.org, did *anyone* with your LSAT score (or lower) get admitted in a past cycle – even just one?

The reason I want you to ask these questions is because I think it is a common misconception that your LSAT score doesn't matter at all when you're a transfer student. While that score definitely matters *much less* than it would if you were applying as a 1L, many schools still look at it and use it (even if just slightly) when determining whether you will be offered admission as a transfer student. Granted, your 1L grades usually matter *the most*, followed by letters of recommendation (if required), your personal statement (which as a transfer student should focus on your vision for yourself post law school and how the school you're applying to will help you achieve that vision for yourself), and your resume. But trailing at the end of that list is still your LSAT score.

Appendix A: Sample Law School Report

Your Ticket In – Akiesha Anderson

Law School Report

Applicant Name: **Akiesha Anderson**
Update Reason:

For: **FALL 2020**

Background

Soc Sec #	xxx-xx-xxxx	Completion Date	12/12/20	Institutions Attended	Degree Date	Level	Code
Service Type	CAS	State of Perm Res.	AL	Hobert College	BS 05/2010	U	2294
Birthdate		Age	32	Fairleigh Dickinson University		U	2263
Prev. Name		Ethnicity	Blk	Rutgers U - University Collegel, New Bru		U	2777
		Sex	Female	New Jersey Institutue of Technology	MS 12/2012	G	2513
Undergraduate Major	Mechanical Engineering Engineering - Other						

Code	Year	Notes from Transcript	Code	Year	Note from Transcript
2294	09-10	Acad Honors. Rank 47 / 492	2263 -	2020	Financial Obligation
2263	08-09	Academic Action			
2777	05-06	Unacknowledged Transcript			
2513	04-05	Term. Action			

Degree School

Percentage of LSAT	95 and up	90-94	85-89	80-84	75-79	70-74	65-60	60-54	55-59	50-54	45-40	40-44	35-30	30-34	25-29	20-24	0-19
	2	3	5	7	6	8	7	3	5	8	10	4	4	10	3	6	9

Percentage Distribution of GPAs	4.00. Up.	3.80. 3.90.	3.60 3.79	3.40. 3.59	3.20. 3.39.	3.00 3.19	2.80. 2.99.	2.60 2.79	2.40. 2.59.	2.20 2.39	2.00. 2.19.	1.80 1.99	1.60. 1.79.	1.59 Down			
	1	1	4	10.	5	23	8.	17	15	11	4	1	0	0			

Transcript Analysis

Year			06-07	07-08	08-09	09-09	09-10	11-12
Education Level			U	U	U	U	U	G
College			Rutgers U	Rutgers U	Fairleigh Dickinson	Hobert College	Hobert College	NJINTEC
College Code			2777	2777	2263	2294	2294	2513
LSAT College Mean			INSF	34	148		151	
Num. Candidates			INSF	374	182		132	
Semester Hours			16.0	28.0	24.0	19.8	33.0	
GPA			3.21	1.76	3.33	3.11	3.43	
Cum. GPA/College			3.21	1.76	3.33	3.11	3.31	SEE
Cum. GPA Percentile Rank			INSF	11	491		821	TRANS
GPA College Mean			INSF	3.20	3.30		2.88	
Cum. Across GPA			3.21	2.29	2.66	2.76	2.94	

Grades Earned	Total		NUMBER OF SEMESTER HOURS BY GRADE FOR EACH SCHOOL - DATE - PERIOD					
3.50 & Up		A	36.5	8.0	0.0	12.0	3.3	13.2
2.50 - 3.49		B	55.0	6.0	8.0	8.0	13.2	19.8
1.50- 2.49		C	19.3	0.0	12.0	4.0	3.3	0.0
0.50 - 1.49		D	2.0	2.0	0.0	0.0	0.0	0.0
0.49 - Down		F	8.0	0.0	8.0	0.0	0.0	0.0
Uncoverted			0.0	0.0	0.0	0.0	0.0	0.0
Total			120.8	16.0	28.0	24.0	19.8	33.0

Summary

LSAT Score Data

Score Band	Score	Percent Rank	Admin. Date	Index
155-161	158	77	10/20	
154-160	157	73	10/19	
			02/19	
			12/18	
159-165	162	88	09/18	
158-160	159		Average	

Undergraduate Summary

Degree (Summary) GPA	3.31	Cumulative GPA	2.94
Semester Hours	52.8	Semester Hours	120.8

Nonpunitive "NC", "WI", and "Repeated" Course Credit Hours

Letters of Recommendation

Number of letters included in this report: 2

Law School Matriculation

Prior law school matriculation or intent to matriculate reported by:

2018 UNIVERSITY OF ALABAMA

Misconduct or Inreggularity Determination

YES   Report Attached

Score Band					
120	130	140	160	170	180
			< >		
Lower =158		Average Score = 159		Upper -162	

Source: SUNY Empire State College, Prelaw Resources, "Example of Law School Report", https://www.esc.edu/prelaw/application-process/example-report/ ; last visted Dec. 12, 2020 (report slightly modified from original version)

Appendix B: Sample Law School Writing Sample

Writing Sample Topic

Directions

The scenario presented below describes two choices, either one of which can be supported on the basis of the information given. Your essay should consider both choices and argue for one over the other, based on the two specified criteria and the facts provided. There is no "right" or "wrong" choice: a reasonable argument can be made for either.

Topic

BLZ Stores, an established men's clothing retailer with a chain of stores in a major metropolitan area, is selecting a plan for expansion. Using the facts below, write an essay in which you argue for one of the following plans over the other based on the following two criteria:

- The company wants to increase its profits.
- The company wants to ensure its long-term financial stability.

The "national plan" is to open a large number of men's clothing stores throughout the country over a short period of time. In doing this, the company would incur considerable debt. It would also have to greatly increase staff and develop national marketing and distribution capabilities. Many regional companies that adopted this strategy increased their profits dramatically. A greater number tried and failed, suffering severe financial consequences. BLZ is not well known outside its home area. Research indicates that the BLZ name is viewed positively by those who know it. National clothing chains can offer lower prices because of their greater buying power. BLZ currently faces increasingly heavy competition in its home region from such chains.

The "regional plan" is to increase the number and size of stores in the company's home region and upgrade their facilities, product quality, and service. This could be achieved for the most part with existing cash reserves. These upgrades would generally increase the prices that BLZ charges. In one trial store in which such changes were implemented, sales and profits have increased. The local population is growing. BLZ enjoys strong customer loyalty. Regional expansion could be accomplished primarily using BLZ's experienced and loyal staff and would allow

Writing Sample Answer

In order to increase its profits and ensure its long-term financial stability, BLZ should move forward with a "regional plan" rather than a "national plan".

The regional plan is a more prudent choice for several reasons. First, because BLZ is not well-known outside of its home area, it is likely unable to compete on a national level. Thus, the national plan is not a good option for it to pursue. While one could argue that the national plan, if successful, could lead to dramatically increased profits for BLZ; the majority of regional companies that attempt to expand nationally, fail - so the likelihood of a local business (like BLZ) being successful in such an attempt is likely to be much lower. Unfortunately, these risks associated with this plan and likelihood of it causing BLZ to go into substantial debt, if not close altogether, simply is not in alignment with BLZ's attempt to ensure its long term financial stability.

In contrast, the regional plan will allow BLZ to achieve both of its goals. By allowing BLZ to increase the number and size of its current stores, it can be assumed that they will naturally experience increased profits as a result. The upgrades that BLZ could implement under this plan would also lead to increased profits. While it is arguable that these profits would not be as dramatic as the profits that could be experienced with a national expansion, the fact that these profits do not come at the risk of financial ruin makes this the better option. Thus, by pursuing the regional expansion plan, BLZ will be able to both ensure its financial stability and increase profits.

For these reasons, BLZ should move forward with a "regional plan" rather than a "national plan".

Appendix C: LOR Template

Here is a list of things that you may want to write your recommender a sentence about and send to them or to simply ask them to touch upon in your letter.

Of course, all these things don't have to be mentioned, but these are some things that may best highlight your qualifications and ability to succeed in law school.

Your:
- Intellect and native intelligence
- Work performance
- Analytical skills and reasoning ability
- Written communication skills
- Oral communication skills
- Independence of thought and creativity
- Quality of work product
- Work ethic and self-discipline
- Enthusiasm and dedication
- Character and ethics
- Maturity and common sense
- Leadership potential
- Potential for the study of law
- Cooperativeness, ability to work with others, and concern for others

To the extent that your recommender has anything to say about these things (or to the extent that you can give them one-liners about any of these) I'm sure that they will serve as an aide in helping to make your letter stellar.

Appendix D: LOR Samples

<u>Sample One: Professional LOR (Above Average)</u>

September 8, 2021

To Whom It May Concern:

RE: Christopher [Last Name Redacted]

I have known Chris since 2014 when he was a student at the East College. He worked on my re-election campaign in 2014 and has worked on other campaigns since then. He has been and continues to be involved in community initiatives designed to empower the Latino community in the political and civic arenas. Through my many years of working with Chris, I have found him to be <u>a focused, dedicated, and responsible young man</u> who <u>maintains a positive attitude</u> and <u>works well with others.</u> He is a <u>self-starter</u> and a <u>consummate professional</u> that innovates to accomplish those duties and obligations he is responsible for.

As a student volunteer and now as a young professional, Chris has held several important positions and distinctions, with a few noted below:

- Digital Media Specialist for Voto Latino, a national organization whose purpose is to educate and empower Latinos about the importance of their vote and register them to vote
- Digital Communication Campaign Strategist for NE State Representative Victoria Neave
- North Nebraska LULAC District Director
- 2014 LULAC National Young Man of the Year
- Nebraska Weekly's 20 Millennials to Watch

85

Chris <u>excels in many areas</u> – academically, community involvement, and workforce professional – to name a few. <u>He brings his *"si se puede"* (it can be done) attitude to everything he is involved in.</u> He has had nothing handed to him; rather, he <u>has worked for all that he has accomplished thus far.</u> He is a <u>well-rounded, balanced individual</u> who will make an excellent student in law school and an excellent lawyer. Because of his background, he can relate to first-generation families; because of his work experience and community involvement, he is able to relate to many levels of society, from the poorest poor to the professional and governing class. Should he be accepted into law school, he will bring keen insight to sectors of our society that few possess. He is <u>a remarkable, accomplished young</u> man who will be a true asset to whatever school he decides to attend.

Yours truly,

[Name Redacted]

Assessment: This is a wonderful letter! Underlined above are all the things that I would have likely taken note of if I were to receive this / still working in admissions. Overall, I would rate this a 4 out of 5 (we graded letters on a scale of 1-5 with 5s being very rare but given out only in instances where a recommender quantifies the applicant in a comparative way, e.g. "this is the BEST young person I've ever worked with" or "he is the top 5% of all students I have worked with.") Also worth noting, I'd recommend asking recommenders to leave dates off of your letters. That way if you reapply or use the letter a few years from now, you don't have to worry about having that older date on it.

Sample Two: Academic LOR (Stellar!)

Letter of Recommendation for Christopher [Last Name]:

To Whom It May Concern,

It is my distinct pleasure to recommend Christopher for admittance. Christopher has taken 5 classes with me and performed at an excellent level in each course. I believe that his high academic level, as well as his desire to achieve success, will make him an ideal candidate for admittance.

As one of my students, Christopher demonstrated the skills necessary for success in an academic environment. Not only did he earn an A for my classes, but he never missed a class session. He actively participated in classroom discussions as well as serving as a leader to other students in the class. He has a great GPA and a success driven personality. I think his greatest asset is his adaptability. He faces any challenge with a can-do attitude and utilizes setbacks and obstacles as learning opportunities.

Christopher also possesses strong desire to serve the public. He volunteered in many social organizations and political campaigns – not to build personal connections, but to serve a community that he believed to be historical disadvantaged. I have no doubt that Christopher will be elected to public office in the near future.

I believe Christopher to be one of my best students ever. I have no doubt that he will truly be a success in any endeavor he may undertake. It is with this in mind that I fully endorse Christopher. If you have any questions, you may reach me at [contact information redacted].

Sincerely,

[Signature Redacted]

Assessment: This is a wonderful letter! Underlined above are all the things that I would have likely taken note of if I were to receive this / still working in admissions. Overall, I would rate this a 5 out of 5 (we graded letters on a scale of 1-5 with 5s being very rare but given out in instances where a recommender quantifies the applicant in the way that yours did here: "one of my best students ever.")

Sample Three: Professional LOR (Average)

February 15, 2022

To Whom It May Concern:

I supervise Christopher at [Employer Redacted] as our Communications Director. [Employer Redacted] is a Nebraska based non-profit fighting to improve working conditions for low-wage workers, with a strategic focus on the construction industry. In his time with our organization, Christopher's commitment to racial and economic justice for working families in Nebraska is evident in his every day work to elevate our mission to new heights. In his role at Workers Defense, he has played a critical role in our campaigns at the local, state, and federal level to advance policies that protect workers and stop harmful legislation by harnessing and leveraging media power. I see daily that he is <u>relentless</u> in his efforts to change hearts and minds through the power of communications and narrative work.

Some of Christopher's accomplishments at [Employer Redacted] and in the broader Nebraska progressive movement include:

- Being a core member of our legislative team that successfully defeated Senate Bill 14, a sweeping preemption bill, in 2021 during the 87th Nebraska Legislative Session that would have forever changed

90

the political landscape of Nebraska by tying the hands of local elected officials from passing local workplace protections like rest breaks for construction workers, non-discrimination ordinances, fair chance hiring, and more.

- Supporting efforts to launch multi-million dollar mutual aid campaigns to provide direct financial assistance to families like the Nebraska Undocu Worker Fund for workers excluded from federal stimulus packages during the COVID-19 pandemic and the Power Up Nebraska Fund for families who were left without basic necessities like water and power during the Winter Storm Uri crisis in 2021 that saw the collapse of the Nebraska energy grid.

- Working alongside our electoral team to run field programs and campaigns to elect progressive candidates across Nebraska like Jose Garza for Travis County District Attorney, Lina Hidalgo for Harris County Judge, Greg Casar for Nebraska Congressional District 35, and more.

Christopher's impact can be felt across the state with millions of workers who have benefitted from having his brilliance on our team as we aim to keep building power for workers who continue to be exploited by systems that oppress them. I know he will make an excellent law student and lawyer one day having been on the frontlines of necessary change that would be impossible without his expertise and dedication. <u>Any institution</u>

would be lucky to have Christopher as a student and eventual graduate because of his unique lens into how laws impact the daily lives of workers and what it takes to build a government that works for working people.

Sincerely,

Signature Redacted, *Communications Director*

Assessment: Notice that there was not much underlined this time. Unfortunately, while all good things are shared in this letter, an admissions committee looks moreso to your resume to determine successes like these. LORs are used slightly different. On a scale of 1 to 5 I would give this letter a 3 (which is average).

Sample Four: Professional LOR (Average)

To Whom It May Concern:

It has come to my attention that Chris is applying to Law School. I have know Chris for over 10 years, both in our involvement with LULAC and other Nebraska community and civil rights activities.

Chris has demonstrated <u>strong leadership skills</u> in the capacities he has been either elected or appointed to. He is <u>thoughtful, committed and very loyal to his community</u>. I have seen him with Dallas civic leaders, elected officials, and community activists. He has been effective and had a great impact on our younger generation of Latinos in Dallas.

I have no reservations in recommending Chris to law school since he has such a strong commitment to change and our democratic process. He will someday become a very effective lawyer, taking all these skills and abilities to help the disenfranchised and poor of our community.

Cordially,

Assessment: This is a decent letter. Underlined above are all the things that I would have likely taken note of if I were to receive this / still working in admissions. Overall, I would rate this a 3 out of 5 as well (we graded letters on a scale of 1-5 with 3s being "good but average"- most letters we received were 3s, so having letters that are 4s or 5s is really impressive.

Sample Five: Professional LOR (Stellar!)

Dear Sir or Madam,

For the last three and a half years Daniel has been working full time at our mortgage company as a licensed mortgage loan officer. <u>In the 23 years that I have been managing and supervising loan officers, none have impressed me more than Daniel</u>. He started at the company as a telemarketer with zero experience in mortgage lending or finance. Within months he took the initiative, on his own, to study and get licensed as a mortgage loan officer; an undertaking that requires passage with over 75% of the National Mortgage Licensing System (NMLS) exam. This test has a historically low passage rate of 57% for first time test takers. Even more amazing is the fact that he accomplished this while raising an infant on his own. His daughter was a mere 6 months old when Daniel came to work for us. Frankly, his <u>determination and his drive to succeed are unparalleled.</u> Early on, I could see he was talented but he <u>completely blew us away when he broke the company's 32 year long record for the most loans originated by a new licensee</u>. He never had the advantage of listening and learning from his experienced colleagues in the office, as he has worked from home since the beginning. He relied solely on conversations with me over the phone and his own ability to read and research the mortgage guidelines and laws governing our industry. All this from an employee we originally hired as a telemarketer!

A mortgage transaction is a complex financial transaction. It is the single largest financial transaction an individual makes in their lifetime. For this reason, a good loan officer has to be <u>intelligent, inquisitive, and responsible</u>. They must be able to operate in an environment that has zero tolerance for violations. Daniel possesses all these qualities and more. He exercises sound credit and risk judgment in recommending loans for approval. He does a thorough assessment of client needs and is excellent at negotiating the best loan transaction for them. He <u>exhibits a high level of professionalism at all times</u> even with clients that he has serviced before and who are loyal to his.

Daniel is strategic in how he operates. Many times he speaks with borrowers who appear not to qualify. They tell his how they have been rejected by numerous companies. The majority of loan officers in the business today will rush these borrowers off the phone immediately, some will even hang up on them. Daniel takes the time to assess their situation and looks for alternative ways he can get them qualified. Many times he succeeds. The times he doesn't, he calls me to see if there's anything I might know that will help his qualify his borrower. He is relentless in his commitment to his borrowers. It is rare in this fast-paced business for a loan officer to treat a prospective borrower with such care. This is a quality that allows his to capture more business than the average loan officer.

I knew Daniel spoke Spanish when I hired him but he has really translated his language skills to a level above and beyond my expectations. He not only has complete mastery of the language, he is able to explain the complex terminology of finance to his Spanish speaking borrower's with ease in a way that they can understand and are comfortable with. He has a deep understanding of the Spanish culture that has allowed his to connect with borrowers in a way the company hasn't been able to before. <u>The relationship he builds with his Spanish speaking borrowers is unbreakable. They trust him completely</u> and refer their family members to him regularly. We rely on his to help us serve this important community and he does not let us down.

<u>Working with Daniel is a rewarding experience with his positive attitude, upbeat personality and with being a great teammate. His attitude is infectious</u>, which is a big thing in a sales environment. I appreciate it every time we speak, as do his fellow Loan Officers. <u>I highly recommend Daniel, from a personal level, but most importantly from a professional level</u>. I firmly believe he will succeed in any environment he puts himself in.

Regards,

[Signature redacted]

Assessment: This is a stellar letter! Underlined above are all the things that I would have likely taken note of if I were to receive this / still working in admissions. Overall, I would rate this a 5 out of 5.

<u>Sample Six: Professional LOR (Stellar!)</u>

6 October 2021

Dear Committee,

May this message find you well.

I am pleased to submit this letter of recommendation for Mr. Williams in support of his application to law school. I have known Mr. Williams for five years, and <u>he was one of my most engaged and well-rounded students</u>. Though Pennsylvania State University routinely boasts excellence as a habit, I am thoroughly impressed with how Mr. Williams embodies our motto and has cultivated an undergraduate experience that has well-prepared him for the challenges and unexpected contours of law school.

Mr. Williams has a clear vision of how he intends to use passion for racial justice to become a civil rights lawyer and enhance the lives of marginalized individuals and communities. Rooted in transformative personal experiences with family and community members, he fluidly permeates the boundaries between the personal and professional in a way that maintains the intimacy of the former and the integrity of the latter. I was often impressed by how he balanced logical reasoning with lyrical prose in his assignments, and I believe this is a skill that will serve him well in his future legal practice. Additionally, his ability to consider matters in a way that not only concerns research methods but also ethics in legal research demonstrates that he is conversant in a number of discourses within and external to his specific disciplines.

Mr. Williams <u>is brilliant, insightful, determined, compassionate, and delightfully humorous</u>—all useful assets when interacting with people of diverse backgrounds. On the first day of class, I knew that he would be an integral part of the cohort. He <u>always arrived prepared to work, spoke confidently, and was friendly toward his classmates, even ones with whom he was unfamiliar.</u> His assertive and inviting personality ideally positioned him as a facilitator during classroom discussions. Consequently, students naturally looked to him to analyze disparate parts of arguments and help provide a cohesive narrative at the end of each session.

Mr. Williams skillfully inserts his voice by carefully listening and then offering an enthusiastic delivery of ideas that clearly indicates his ability to absorb new information, analyze theories, and contribute to robust discourse. For example, I once had the deep honor of witnessing him skillfully redirect a particularly difficult student who had successfully riled up several other classmates. Whereas his peers had become aggravated beyond a point of listening to the gentleman, he deftly and firmly interject and pointed out the numerous fallacies in the other gentleman's argument. His confident response disarmed the antagonist and demonstrated to others how to handle someone who had become intentionally confrontational while feigning a thin veneer of respectability. This stands out to me because, as a legal professional, he will have to navigate a variety of personalities, from outright confrontational individuals to those who prefer smooth condescension. After witnessing Mr. Williams skillfully disrupt the gentleman and quickly dismantle his arguments, I am confident that he <u>is equipped to deescalate any tension</u> that may arise when encountering people in heightened states of aggravation.

Mr. Williams has ambitious ideas about how he intends to move through the world and positively impact his communities. He <u>has the intellect, heart, and soul of a philosopher, orator, and community organizer</u>. He brings his full attention to every task, and he does not shy away from a challenge. In fact, he actively courts new opportunities to grow. He came to class prepared with his own questions and clear ideas about how to pursue the answers. Furthermore, <u>when I set a bar, he often pushed it higher</u>. These qualities will serve him well in a law program where it is necessary to be self-motived and self-governing while navigating a new set of academic and social conditions. <u>Students like him are a reminder of why I entered this profession—to cultivate scholars and encourage them to become well-rounded individuals.</u>

<u>It is impossible to overstate the impact that Mr. Williams had on our class and on me as a professional</u>. I have not written this recommendation lightly. As a Black woman mentored by an uncle who passed the Mississippi state bar during an era rife with racial discrimination, I have a great deal of respect for young Black professionals who choose to enter this important profession. Mr. Williams embodies an admirable blend of the qualities I've seen in the most successful lawyers who remain rooted in their communities. His application clearly indicates capacity, promise, and a robust research agenda. His clarity of purpose, coupled with his boundless potential, demonstrate that he is well-poised to thrive in law school. <u>I fully believe that, when we encounter young men like Mr. Williams, it is our duty to ensure that they go as far as their intellect and talent can carry them</u>. If honored with acceptance into your program, he will excel and be a positive reflection of the institution's highest ideals.

Thank you for your time and attention. If there are any questions about my full support of his application, please do not hesitate to contact me via [contact info redacted] for further conversation.

Warm regards,

[Signature redacted]

Assessment: This is another stellar letter! Underlined above are all the things that I would have likely taken note of if I were to receive this / still working in admissions. Overall, I would rate this a 5 out of 5. Although the professor did not use a numerical value to describe the student, via various things she writes it is clear that she thinks of this student as the kind of academic that is very rare to come across.

<u>Sample Seven: Professional LOR (Above Average)</u>

October 13, 2021

Law School Admissions Council
662 Penn Street
PO Box 8508
Newtown, PA 18940-8508

RE: Applicant Monica Riley

Dear Law School Admissions Council:

I write in support of the application of Monica Riley for admission to law school. I have taught hundreds of undergraduate and law students and supervised many in internships. I taught courses in Legal Process, Statutory Law and Legal Ethics at the Santa Barbara College of Law. I have taught a course entitled "Law and Civil Rights" during 10 quarter terms in the Chicana/o Studies Department at the University of California at Los Angeles. I have taught the same basic course twice in the Political Science Department and once as an Interdisciplinary course at UCLA entitled "Latina/os and the American Legal System" or "Latina/os and American Law".

Monica Riley has served as an intern in my law office beginning in January 2021. She has been primarily engaged in assisting myself and an immigration law specialist. Ms. Riley <u>has been instrumental</u> in assisting the legal effort to obtain humanitarian relief for our client and in managing the widespread media attention attendant to the case. She <u>has demonstrated a quick understanding of the legal issues in this novel case</u> and is consistently ahead-of-the-game in managing the public interest mechanics at issue. Ms. Riley is very bright and engaging. She is extremely diligent in seeking out tasks which further the overall effort and in taking the point in accomplishing the endeavor. She takes direction well, demonstrates uncanny initiative and works to successful conclusion. The end product in tasks she undertakes is always extraordinary.

Ms. Riley is highly motivated and fully committed to engaging in a course of legal studies. She has extraordinary verbal and written communication skills which will serve her well in law school and thereafter. I expect that Ms. Riley will leave an indelible mark at the law school she chooses to attend and will become a high-quality practitioner of the law. She is uniquely well-prepared and strongly motivated to take on the rigors of law school studies. I have no doubt that she will become a credit to our profession.

Sincerely,

[Sincerely redacted]

Assessment: This is a really good letter. Underlined above are all the things that I would have likely taken note of if I were to receive this / still working in admissions. Overall, I would rate this a 4 out of 5 as well (we graded letters on a scale of 1-5 with 4s being "above average"- most letters we received were 3s, so having letters that are 4s or 5s is really impressive.

Appendix E: Personal Statement Samples

<u>Sample One: Future Civil Rights Attorney</u>

At only seventeen years old, my uncle was detained and beaten for a crime he did not commit. I began reading my uncle's case file at the age of sixteen and was shocked to find out the truth behind his arrest. The prosecution's case relied solely on the testimony of an officer with a vendetta and an eyewitness who recanted his testimony, admitting that the officer paid him to pin a murder on my uncle. Nearly twenty years after his conviction, an appellate court vacated it, ordered a retrial, and released my uncle on bail. After serving twenty-three years for a crime he did not commit, he was finally freed.

My uncle was not the only family member I lost to the prison system. At six years old, I found myself sitting in an imposing courtroom of mahogany and marble. I watched as a judge sentenced my father to ten years in federal prison. I watched tears fall from my father's eyes and did not even get the chance to embrace him just one last time before uniformed officers led him away in shackles – a memory permanently ingrained in my mind. Although my father was the one convicted, I too felt the heavy burden of his sentence.

As a child, I always wanted to know who the powerful man who took my father away from me was. All I remember from that day was that a white man, wearing a black robe, commanded the room like no one I had seen before. I felt voiceless in trying to protect my father's life. At six years old, if I had been given the opportunity, I would have told the judge that I was losing an integral part of my life and my development as a Black man. But I never had a chance to say those things before he was taken away from me. His absence presented me with responsibilities and challenges I could never have foreseen, such as anxiety and a damaged sense of self-confidence. His absence also taught me how to challenge the racial hatred that haunts my community to this very day. Shouldering these responsibilities and overcoming these challenges has led me to find my purpose and voice for other disenfranchised people.

My desire to fight for marginalized communities inspired my drive to pursue a legal career in civil rights. That drive became even more personal one week before my high school graduation when my father's fear of my own potential incarceration almost became a reality. As I ran home late from a student government meeting, I saw lights flashing behind me, and my heart began to pump in my chest. Chicago police officers ordered me to stop and aggressively began to frisk me. The officers warned me not to move and asked me if I had any weapons. I replied that I only had my library books. According to them, I "fit the description" of the Black male suspect they were seeking. As I was lying across the hood of a police car in handcuffs, I felt like I could not say anything to save myself. Among the many thoughts racing through my mind was the terrifying reminder of the many Black men who did not make it out of this situation alive. At that moment, when my father's most significant fear could have become a reality, the officers released me. I was shaken, confused, and angry at what had happened to me. I then recognized that the books in my hands were perhaps the most potent weapons I could wield against this system of racial profiling and harassment.

As a first-generation college student, attending law school is about becoming a voice for others and breaking a cycle of voicelessness. My father's and my uncle's experiences with the criminal justice system powerfully demonstrated why going to law school is imperative for me. Although my uncle has been freed, his legal battle and plight to be exonerated are not over. I now work for the firm handling my uncle's case, and I hope to someday be able to exonerate and defend others like him.

Sample Two: Future Technology Law Attorney

"Globalization ought to be valued over Protectionism." Fifty-one times during my final year of high school debate, this was the resolution on the table. Each time, I declared "I am proud to negate" – and I was. As I passionately condemned the World Trade Organization for its persistent failure to protect vulnerable groups from exploitation and neglect, it might have seemed to my opponents that I was merely playing the part well. But my position on protectionism had long been in gestation, years before I stood behind any podium. My instinct to protect the vulnerable was born of a childhood spent in three separate homes.

I didn't live long in my first home. My father was serving four years in prison; my mother, despite working from sunrise to sunset, couldn't afford a babysitter for my sisters and me. One day, my youngest sister was hungry for breakfast. I decided to walk her to the gas station to get cereal. We strolled down the street, my hand on her back as she hung on my hip. I knew my sister needed someone to watch out for her; I was going to be that person. But I was just five years old; she was two. A neighbor called Child Protective Services and we were ultimately handed over to our grandparents by the court.

My second home was stable, at least on paper. My grandparents promoted safety – measures were quickly put in place to make sure I didn't walk to any other gas stations alone. But two adults and strict rules aren't always enough; a child needs love too. Unfortunately, by age twelve, it was clear to me that this crucial element was lacking. On countless occasions, I'd wake up to entire bottles of "holy" oil having been dumped on my face by my grandmother. She would also throw penetrating words and blunt objects at my sister, as well as frequently refuse to take my grandfather to his dialysis appointments. I knew then who I was quickly becoming: a protector. I spent innumerable late nights helping my sister work through her dyslexia and complete her homework. I got up three mornings a week to dress my grandfather for his dialysis, watching as dementia took dominion over his mind. I committed myself to keeping others safe. But when I was fifteen, my grandmother sought to vacate her temporary custody. I was returned to my mother, but my sisters were left in my grandmother's care.

My third home was loving but lacked stability. Despite my mother and I both working, money was still tight. Eventually, my mother began a relationship with a man who promised her financial stability. It wasn't long before physical abuse and death threats became a recurring theme in our home. There I stood late one Saturday night face to face with him as he carried a loaded shotgun hunting for my mother. The relationship ended that night, but I learned that being a protector requires an immense amount of courage. Somehow, I convinced him to hand over the gun.

By the time I joined Speech and Debate, my natural desire to protect had evolved into an unshakeable passion for justice. With every debate case I presented, I stood in the shoes of my younger self. I fought not only for protectionist policies, but also for the fair treatment of my younger sisters, my grandpa, my mother. Speech and Debate encouraged me to look beyond the scope of my debate resolution and childhood homes in search for unique pathways of protecting others.

At the age of eighteen, my search led me to Washington, DC, where I worked as a summer intern for a congressman serving on the Subcommittee on Courts, Intellectual Property, and the Internet. As I began conducting research for the representative. In the halls of the nation's capitol, far removed from the events and places of my childhood, I discovered new outlets for my protective impulses. I was instantly infatuated with the power of technology and the ways it could foster a safer, more equitable society. In 2019, I started working as a Solutions Specialist at Verizon Communications and witnessed how working-class communities in rural areas continuously lose internet access and cellular service, largely resulting from the 2018 FCC repeal of net neutrality. As of this writing, I am spending summer 2021 in London working as a legal intern for Bark & Co., where I am reviewing cases involving cryptocurrency fraud and coming to better understand the wide-ranging implications of insufficient protection of digital property.

I've developed a keen interest in the legal gray areas surrounding increasingly ubiquitous technological developments. I believe that minimizing these grey areas concerning certain existing and emerging technologies is essential to protecting individuals who otherwise would be disproportionately harmed by the major implications of insufficient protection of digital property. I am eager to embark on a legal career dedicated to shining light on these gray areas.

I have been a protector my entire life. I will continue fighting to protect the vulnerable – be it behind podiums, in courtrooms, in boardrooms, in chambers, or at your law school.

Sample Three: Future Federal Prosecutor

My home in Yuma, Arizona is less than two miles from the Mexican border. Just beyond the border, the city on the other side, is home to some of the world's most brutal drug cartels. This otherwise benign stretch of desert is ground zero in the war on drugs. Growing up, I would read every detail and see every picture of unfathomable violence taking place between the two cities. Although the majority of the violence that filled the newspapers occurred across the border, I learned from a young age that these gruesome events occur on this side of the border too.

I was five-years-old when the realities of border town life destroyed my childhood innocence. The evening started like any other on a warm, dry February night. My family gathered at my abuela's house for a Carne Asada—the deafening sound of cumbias and mouth-watering aroma of fajitas filled the air, as I assembled makeshift forts with my cousins out of old blankets and lawn chairs. Upon returning home from our raucous evening, we found a peculiar elephant statue with a note signed by a close family friend, Sam, on the doorstep of our mobile home. In my community, an elephant statute serves as a good luck charm, but we did not understand the reason for its presence at our home.

In the middle of the night, a bone-rattling phone call provided all the answers. The call explained that the cartel had executed Sam and burned his body. Sam, who was involved in the drug trade, must have known that his time was short. That also meant his friends could endure the same fate. Although my dad was never involved in the drug trade, as Sam's friend, the cartel would view him as a loose end to tie up. We needed luck now more than ever.

My dad frantically barked orders to pack up our belongings. Suddenly, he gave me a tearful hug, ran out the door, and sped off in his truck, alone. I did not know whether I would see him again. But before I could consider the moment, my sister whisked me outside into my mom's Honda-turned-getaway-car. We hurried to a safe haven while I ducked behind books stacked against the windows in the backseat, praying desperately that everything would be okay.

The next day, my dad returned distraught and broken. The police had interrogated him overnight for hours, demanding he provide responses to unanswerable questions. They showed him pictures of what was left of his best friend. The ordeal frightened my dad enough to move us into hiding until the situation cooled down. Even when my family emerged, we did not truly feel safe. For years, I looked over my shoulder wondering if the cartel sat in that passing car or whether the stranger at the corner was surveilling us.

After surviving the fear that consumed my childhood, I continued to see the impact of the drug trade first-hand. In high school, the cartel murdered one of my friends who had fallen into a destructive lifestyle. The stories from the newspaper were an all too real portion of my daily life. I responded with sadness, anger, and frustration. I did not know what I could do to end this cycle of violence. At times, I just wanted to forget it all and leave this world behind. My dream became to leave Yuma and start a new life. College became my means of escape.

When I moved away for college, I thought I left behind the mental torture of my youth. But I could not simply forget my past and do nothing about it. No matter how far I go, the border town will always be a part of me. I therefore resolved to use my opportunities to improve life for Yuma and its people. So I accepted a job upon graduation as a paralegal with the U.S. Attorney's Office in my home state. Every day, I support the office's efforts to combat the violent narcotics trade and hold those accountable who inflict damage on my community. Next, I hope to prepare for a career pursuing justice in turbulent areas. I look forward to furthering my understanding of cross-border conflict and improving opportunity for people through the Human Rights Institute, which makes your law school best suited to my personal and professional goals.

Sample Four: Future Public Interest Attorney

At the age of 15, I sat nervously in the front office of my high school waiting impatiently for my grandmother to deliver some news to me. The lady at the front desk spoke in a slow and caring tone to my grandmother, "Yes ma'am, I understand, he is here waiting, I can give him the phone." Those words planted themselves into my mind and rooted me to my seat. The lady at the front desk handed me the phone, and I heard my grandmother speak, "Your mother was in a bad accident at work, she injured her back and—" my mind did not let me listen beyond the first sentence. My grandmother had to take on the financial, emotional, and physical responsibilities of taking care of a high school freshman. My mother injured her spine and became unable to perform basic tasks. She could no longer actively take care of me. As a single, working-class mother, she worked as a warehouse loader, transporting large crates of food products into the back of an 18-wheeler without machines. My mother was unable to provide for me anymore and her legal battle with Workers' Compensation consumed her time for many years to come. With no money to acquire the services of a lawyer, she tried to take on the case herself, but could not adequately represent herself. It quickly became too complex, and she hired a lawyer at her own expense in the middle of her case, which caused the case to continue into multiple years, having yet to end. As a child, I remember being angry at her job and her lawyers for not providing the adequate care she deserved and needed as someone who did not have many resources. The anger gurgling in myself was all-encompassing, affecting my work ethic and focus, so I channeled it into a passion. My circumstances taught me how to use my emotions as a driving force and have given me the motivation to become a public interest lawyer.

Like myself, many people who are in vulnerable positions are one accident away from losing everything. Being in this position for most of my teenage and adult life, I learned what it was like in these positions and the overwhelming emotion of helplessness that becomes frustration, loneliness, and inadequacy. As I grew up, I was told about the plights of the legal battle between my mother and the company she worked for, and all I desired was to help her and I could not. I promised myself since that age that I would never willingly allow others to go through similar pain without the legal services they needed. I desired nothing more than to become someone that could help her and people like her, which led me down a path of community service in college.

After college, I continued my path of service and currently serve with City Year, a member of AmeriCorps, where I shape the lives of children through mentorship, coaching, and tutoring in a holistic approach to their personal, academic, and emotional growth. Immediately prior to my time with City Year, I melded my passion for law and community service by interning at Legal Services of North Florida, which is a non-profit that provides civil legal assistance to low-income and vulnerable populations. Working alongside attorneys, I was more than inspired and wanted to follow the same path of having a balance of technical knowledge and passion in serving others. Through this and other work experiences, I have realized that change is not a large-scale event designed to overhaul old ways of thinking. Rather, change is something done through individual actions or a change in attitude for a day. An education in law will allow me to tap into the societal frameworks to bring positive change in the lives of others – client by client – and support the interests of the public to those that cannot afford, or who feel alienated from our judicial system. As a future public interest attorney, I hope to meet the needs of communities, so the law is not perceived as an exclusionary system that works for some. Many hands carry the work of supporting an individual in any community, and I wish to be an integral part so people can get the services necessary to continue to grow in their lives no matter their age, race, economic status, and other identities they may hold to create a more equitable society.

Sample Five: Future JAG

When my mother became pregnant with me, she dropped out of her senior year of college and, shortly after, married my father. My father, who dropped out of high school, would have it no other way. He used the Bible to teach my two sisters and me that as females we were less valuable than males. My mother's silence offered loud support of his lessons. Episodes of my father's verbal and physical abuse toward my mother and I was common during my formative years. He belittled us and attacked our confidence and our worth. I was a mischievous, high-spirited and, sometimes, defiant child. My sisters, in contrast, learned from my mistakes and, by doing so, were able to largely avoid the physical consequences I received almost daily. Feeling unprotected and alone, I ran away several times. This disrupted the household even more. During my teenage years, a number of dead-end, minimum wage jobs and a failed attempt at college left me feeling desperate, anxiety-ridden and with even less confidence.

A chance encounter with a navy recruiter, Petty Officer Adam Andrews, changed the trajectory of my life. I did not think I was military material but I felt my options were limited. I needed to get out of my parents' home, so I chose the Navy. The best experiences of my life stemmed from that decision. I found balance, stability, and discipline almost immediately. I became more comfortable "in my skin" and began to trust the strength of my own voice. During boot camp, I was chosen to be the Master-at-Arms, a leadership role within the 80-female housing unit. My shipmates referred to me as Andi, a shortened version of my last name, and that just felt right. I have never felt the name "Tonya" fit my personality. To me, "Tonyas" are easy, laid-back, and quiet. Yet I am not easy, laid-back or quiet. I like to talk - a lot - and to write. I value the ability to effectively express my views. I need to have a voice. "Andi" represented, to me, someone who was feisty, interesting, and secure. Because of my father, I was raised in a family where my voice was a nuisance and every feminine idea was treated dismissively or with disdain. The periods of low-confidence throughout my life paralleled periods in which I found myself unable to speak out for myself. Though periods of low-confidence were still evident in my earlier military years, I developed personally and professionally very quickly. Aside from the various awards I received from each command (duty station), my improved confidence was supported by direct acknowledgments from both my leaders and my peers.

At each command, I was selected for leadership roles, well before I had attained the proper qualifications to work in those positions. I was trusted by my chains of command to ensure my teams accomplished all tasks expertly. In such roles, I was the liaison between my superiors and subordinates. I recognized the importance of effective communication. The initiators of the messages or information I passed needed to trust that I was adequately conveying what they wanted to express. Due to my research and writing skills, I was also sought by multiple peers to appeal their Non-judicial Punishment (NJP). I drafted my first appeal within my first six months of service. It was emotion-based and lacked any semblance of legal substance. My attempt at explaining (what I deemed to be) the ridiculousness of the charge was immature and. embarrassing. Unfortunately, for my colleague this was the only appeal I wrote in which the NJP was approved (upheld) by the reviewing authority. I ensured all subsequent appeals for other sailors were based on extensive research, on whether the NJP was unjust or disproportionate, and on the reasons why the NJP was unjust or disproportionate; in essence, the appeals were centered on justice and appropriateness. Even though there was a great amount of risk involved in the legal assistance I provided, I enjoyed the legal research and writing immensely. As a result of my work on later appeals, sailors' cases were dismissed, and all rights restored entirely. These rights included rate, pay, and retention of service (with the ability to later separate with an "Honorable" discharge versus the proposed "Other Than Honorable" discharge); loss of any of these rights would significantly impair a sailor's life. Such opportunities further developed my love of legal processes and inspired me to pursue a career in law.

My military experiences coupled with my undergraduate and graduate studies have naturally developed the foundational skills I need during my pursuit of a career in law. Most importantly, my adult experiences have supported a healthy level of confidence which lends to the strength of my voice. I would like my powerful voice to speak for others when they do not have the voice to speak for themselves or when they feel they are not being heard. When my military career ended, I held onto my feisty identity and my confident voice; I remained Andi.

Sample Six: Future Business Law Attorney

I couldn't understand why we had to move out of my childhood home so suddenly. One minute everything was fine, and the next we were moving into a tiny 2 bedroom apartment. My grandmother did everything she could to make sure my little brother and I had a perfect life. We had amazing holidays with rooms filled with gifts, week long vacations every winter break, and we were enrolled in one of the best private schools in our area. I lived a dream life because of my grandmother's hard work;   a life I never imagined ending.

My grandmother was a DC Metro employee who sought to start her own transportation business. It wasn't until 1996, the year I was born, that she decided to retire from DC Metro, and start her own transportation business. Within 4 years, her company became a thriving local business, having contracts with multiple after school programs, churches, and the government. With the fast growth of her transportation company, she purchased a brand new home for our family. A home I didn't think I would ever have to say goodbye to.

A month before I was to start the 6th grade, she explained to us that things would   be changing rather quickly. I was informed that I would   be going to a different school in a different city. As a child, this was the worst news ever. Emotions of rage and anger filled my body, as I watched the real estate agent give tours of my home to strangers   . Just a few months ago, everything was "normal", at least that's what I thought.

I was afraid to ask her how did we end up in this situation? What happened to the company? Instead I turned my confusion and anger in to a passion for understanding business as a whole. I wanted to learn how to start a successful business as well as retain its success, especially for minority businesses like my grandmother's. This passion of mine motivated me to major in business when the time came for me to go to college.

While in college, I was fortunate enough to take classes that allowed me to dive deep into the business field, from marketing, to

114

actually creating an imaginary company from the ground up. It wasn't until my last semester that   I was introduced to the legal side of business. My Business   Law class opened my eyes to the importance of contracts and rules within a company. You can   have all the marketing and ideas in the world, but without having a strong legal presence, the business will not last.

With my new discovery, I decided to ask my fellow classmates who owned their own businesses, if they had an attorney to assist them. I was shocked to see how many of the minority owned small businesses on my campus lacked legal understanding. How did they expect to make sure no one stole their ideas? How would   their   company prevent potential law   suits? They all had goals of one day expanding their companies, but never thought about the details needed to protect them.

I also saw how many of the minority owned small businesses in my community lacked legal representation. They didn't have someone looking out for their best interest in order to ensure longevity as well as protection for their companies. Business owners need someone who will not only educate them on the steps necessary to develop their business, but also someone who possesses the knowledge needed to secure and protect the company. Attending law school will allow me to gain the knowledge needed to add to my strong business background. · By becoming an attorney, I will be able to make an impact on my community by helping as many small minority owned businesses as possible, to prevent them from experiencing the fate my grandmother did.

Sample Seven: Future Legislative Attorney

Halfway through my internship at the California State Legislature, I was asked to create a memo analyzing five fifty-page carbon fee proposals under consideration during our legislative session – within two hours. This was not unusual – my boss, a senator, would often request briefings on a variety of issues to inform his policies, within a short amount of time. Two hours and a deep dive into our state's budget, existing laws, and environmental and tax policy later, I sent over the memo. My boss was impressed and directed the caucus policy counsel, who would generally provide these memos themselves, to distribute it amongst our entire caucus.

That following week, I was invited to join the senator and his colleagues in a high-level carbon fee strategy meeting. I walked through a hallway lined with portraits of historic Californians and maps of our state's landmarks and mountains – on the right was the Senate Floor, where elected senators spoke on behalf of hundreds of thousands of people. At the end, was a room already filling up with some of the most powerful policymakers in Washington state. The familiar feeling of imposter syndrome exacerbated by my otherness welcomed me into the room, although this time it was accompanied by the heavy weight of decision-making that impacted all Californians – immigrant, LGBTQIA+, working-class, wealthy, Black, and brown alike.

I made three immediate observations upon walking into the meeting room: besides being one of two staffers, the only without a law degree, I was also the only womxn, person of color, and person under 35. Yet, carbon fees do not just affect men, white people, or people 35 or older. Copies of my memo circulated the room, providing the details for discussion, but how the information was interpreted and what interests were represented were beyond my control. Debates began to unfold about where the new revenue would head and who it would come from. While these decisions were supposed to be informed by the constituents that elected each Senator, they were ultimately decided by the individual experiences and beliefs each of these elected officials held. I don't doubt that these older, white, cisgender men could be allies to marginalized communities, but they did not have the intimate understanding of experiences that womxn, communities of color, and younger folks have had with government policies and laws that have destroyed our neighborhoods, scrutinized and policed our bodies, and polluted our futures.

In this moment, while I technically had a seat at the table, I felt that my chair was merely ornamental. As the daughter of Haitian refugees sponsored to America to escape political persecution and chase the American Dream and economic advancement, I felt torn by

116

my duty to show respect and gratitude for the government that saved my family members from the civil war they themselves started and the complicity I demonstrated by sitting silent and upholding the generational cycles of violence directed towards marginalized communities. In the same way that case law has set precedent for *legal* practices of racism, such as racial profiling or no-knock warrants, the accepted beliefs associated with white supremacy, patriarchy, and ageism are weaved into our public consciousness and have set the framework for *socially accepted* racism and injustices—this I witnessed first-hand during the Senate meeting on the proposed carbon fee.

From that meeting on, I couldn't continue to wait for invitations to actively contribute at these tables. I couldn't wait for those in positions of power to recognize my capabilities. I ended my work at the Senate as my senator's top aide and not only joined more strategy meetings, where I engaged in critical conversations, but also wrote legislation. My proposed laws covered 1st Amendment rights in regulating campaign misinformation, reforming felonious conduct bars that precluded the family of decedents from their due process and civil litigation rights, public option healthcare, and mental health access for gun violence survivors. With each piece of legislation I proposed, I sought to center the voices and experiences of historically marginalized communities, a tool I will continue to wield as a civil rights attorney.

The vast structural changes I envision for a more just future exceeded my individual abilities though, so I sought out opportunities where I could strategically build power *across* marginalized communities, in order to change both our government and our society. And if these collaborative opportunities weren't available, I created them: building a collective of BIPOC legislative staffers demanding more from our workplace, as well as creating Haitian Youth Forums, a national organization dedicated to mobilizing and educating Haitian youth. As a future community-based lawyer and advocate, I believe in the power of collective representation as a catalyst for re-envisioning our realities and capabilities.

Sample Eight: Undecided Law Path

"Ms. Jackson, we understand that you are working to pay for school, but your grades have fallen, and we must put you on academic probation. If money is an issue, perhaps you should consider coming back to school when you can afford it. You can always attend college later." These were the words of an academic advisor, on an oddly chilly Friday morning, in Alabama, that I will never forget. They weren't simply written on the screens of an university email; they became engraved in the mind of a 18-year old young lady who simply desired to further her education. *How could this happen to me?* I grew up like several of my peers, in a single parent household, with a mother who beat so many odds and refused to allow her children to be a statistic. When it came to our education, we, her children, were passionate about not simply accomplishing our goals, but making her proud.

I began my collegiate pursuit at the University of North Alabama. It was an opportunity to get away from what was familiar, make new connections and friends, explore a new world, and learn from cultures outside of my own. Honestly, I believed that most of my senior class would end up in jail or prison if they didn't have a plan as soon as graduation was done, and I was determined not to have that same story. I went to the University of North Alabama unaware of the financial strain it would cause my family and me. I was soon placed in a position that forced me to choose between not attending college anymore and paying for my education on my own. In that moment, I once again I decided that not attending college was still not an option.

To fulfill my financial duties in my first year of school, I decided to get a job. It began as a harmless pursuit to assist with my financial obligations at UNA, but soon blossomed into me working two or three jobs to help pay for my fees. I was unfocused in class, late on assignments, lethargic and most days, just simply going through the motions. It became a paper chase, in the name of academics. Eventually, my innocent quest for financial stability landed me on academic probation in 2005. While my mother couldn't give me the world, she gave me what she could. It was my mom who kept encouraging me and even giving to me when she was financially able to. It didn't stop at my mom, my siblings also encouraged and supported me during this process. I learned that the power of presence can be everything when you are trying to reach a goal, and my family definitely possessed that. As amazing as this tangible and emotional support was from my immediate and even extended family, I still struggled with being on this journey. Surely the universe knew my struggle. I was simply attempting to pay my own way through school…after all, I didn't have any other help available to me. *Where did I go wrong? Why did this happen to me?* I had my life all planned out and this was not the perfect story.

Let's fast forward a few years. Walking into the Dallas County felony probation office was just a normal part of my everyday routine that I was so used to doing. However, today was different! Today, I began to notice those who were entering the building and my heart slowly sank. I saw that the majority of those who entered for their weekly/monthly check-ins were racial minorities, whereas the majority of the attorneys/public defenders were not. I started to think about how it has to be hard to have someone fight for your freedom and rights when they look nothing like you and have no idea what it is like to be Black in America. As a Black woman in America, I wrestled with what I could do to bring about change to what I had witnessed that day. Where are the advocates for the voiceless that look like them? A fire that was already started at a young age had then ignited in my soul to begin my journey to become a lawyer. I begin to visualize all the changes I hope to make. I thought of the legacy and the path that I wanted to create as an attorney. I want to be a voice for those who look like me, are from the same economic background and who embrace the fact that being Black in America is an unique experience. I want to be able to help those who are entangled in a system that seemingly was not built to benefit us as a people. I have lived in an era that has allowed me to see the disparities that minorities face; and I have lived in areas where I have been able to witness firsthand the mistreatment or the lack of opportunities that are given to one due to the color of their skin. The bridge has to be created where minorities have the same opportunities

119

in life as their counterparts, including access to legal representation from members of their same ethnic background. With me, the voices of those not heard would be heard.

In retrospect, this journey to law school was not about perfection, it was about perseverance and producing. I realize now that my mother traveled this path as well. She also believed that no matter what path I had to take, she and my family wanted me to attain my goal. I soon realized that my journey was never just about me alone. My journey eventually inspired siblings, family, and friends to have the same experience and motivation to earn higher education degrees. I'm chasing my dream, not simply to inspire my family, but to educate myself and to help those who have had a journey that doesn't look like perfection. They too deserve a chance! The less than stellar grades I received during undergrad are not reflective of my academic ethics nor can they be attributed to the journey I am seeking to begin by obtaining a law degree. It is however, reflective of me learning more about myself and my limits. It is reflective of my will to not give up and to work hard at what is in place. It is reflective of my quest to assist those who don't live in a perfect world, and to become so astute in this field that proper justice is given to every individual—no matter their past. For this experience, for all my experiences, I am better and feel I can be an asset as a law student and future lawyer.

<u>Sample Nine: Future Business Attorney</u>

In the middle of the night, two police officers rushed into our home to search for my sister and me. The officers carried us away while we screamed and cried for our intoxicated mother, who did not understand what happened until the next day. After that night, my sister and me, a seven-year-old, spent the next six years of our lives moving from home to home, leading us to believe we would never amount to anything more than being foster kids.

Nevertheless, I did not lose all hope. My mother was eventually able to move us from Alabama to Georgia. I was very young at the time, and my first night was scary and restless. My mother, my sister, and I stayed on the top floor of a men's shelter because there were no family shelters available to take us in. I slept in a chair because there were no beds, blankets, or pillows. The next day, we were placed into a "21 nights" family shelter.

Staying in a shelter was a new and challenging experience, but I learned to be strong. Every morning we had to leave the shelter by 6 am and could not return until 6 pm. As such, I spent most of my time caring for my little sister while my mom searched for a job, even though it was difficult. Taking on more responsibility in a new environment was challenging, but in my mother's absence, I was all my younger sister had. Thankfully, we found a home, and my mom started a new job, and I went on to attend college.

While in college, I became interested in the legal profession after noticing a lack of minority representation in the legal field. Representation is so important, and I believe that only 5% of U.S. lawyers being Black is a problem. I want to change that. After I noticed a growth of new business ventures starting on social media, I wondered how I could help and be of service. I saw with these new businesses that many of them were not expanding in the way they should have or were failing. To me, this was partly due to a lack of representation. As an attorney, I want to work specifically with new small businesses developed by individuals of color. I want to work with them to handle their legal matters, including securing their business licenses and trademarks correctly the first time around. Eventually, I would like to also be able to help social media influencers and entertainers as I believe they encounter similar issues. Based on my life experiences, like these individuals and businesses, I started from the bottom and have not let failure or obstacles get in the way of my success. I have the determination, motivation, and tenacity to go to law school, be a successful lawyer, and ensure that new small businesses, social media influencers, and entertainers are successful. A law degree will add to that by providing me with the knowledge and help minority business owners while also diversifying the legal profession (and adding to that 5%).

Accordingly, your institution is my ideal school because it offers an intellectual property trademark clinic. This clinic will provide me with the training I need to be an excellent attorney. Participating in this clinic at will allow me to represent individuals and small businesses trying to secure their federal trademark registrations. Working under the direct supervision of adjunct professor and supervising attorney Akiesha Anderson, would be an honor as she has over 20 years of trademark experience, and I believe I would excel under her supervision and learn a lot from her experience. In addition, as someone who has been homeless before, I am especially interested in some of the pro bono opportunities available, including being able to volunteer with your Legal Clinic for the Homeless. Furthermore, your institution has a thriving BLSA chapter and provides easy access to employers I would love to work for. As such, I know that your school is the perfect fit for me, and I would be honored to attend this prestigious institution.

Sample Ten: Future Children's Rights Attorney

I sat in the courtroom lobby, nervously anticipating my first day of on the job training, while skimming through the disturbing history of this case. It was a chilly February afternoon, and here I was, about to walk into the courtroom, not knowing what lied ahead for Christian, the juvenile and defendant of this case. The report revealed possible issues with the case from well over 5 years ago. You did not have to be an attorney to understand some of the incidents in this case were unethical and disturbing. Christian was abandoned by his mother at the age of 3 to a woman who ended up abandoning him at juvenile hall after initially accusing him of assaulting her daughter when he was 11. She later recanted her story. However, he was sent to sit in juvenile detention until he was 16 because no family members could be located and because his then lawyer allowed Christian to plead guilty by signing a statement that implicated him. Inexplicably, this case was in conjunction with the Department of Child and Family Services case, which was the one I was training for as a Court Appointed Special Advocate (CASA).

The events described in the case report made it clear that Christian's counsel did not properly assist him. This was also evident by the tone he took when Christian attempted to question him regarding his case and possible adoption. Christian seemed to not understand the case and proceedings. The judge in that particular case, sentenced Christian to 20 years in prison, without evidence and any witnesses; solely on the basis of a document that Christian was made to sign by his attorney without fully understanding the ramifications. As a result, Christian was sentenced as an adult, despite still being a minor and after sitting in jail for over 6 years because he no longer had family that could care for him. There was no way of swaying the judge's ruling as she made it clear that she would not listen to anyone's opinion. With our efforts, we had hoped to have been able to keep him in the care of the Department of Children and Family Services until he turned 18. However, on this day, the judge felt that was no longer necessary, and ordered Christian to be removed from children services and be viewed as an adult to carry on his sentence even though he was still a minor.

I was fortunate to be sitting there listening and observing that case as well as being involved in others while being appointed as a CASA for my county's Family Court division. This experience only deepened my conviction that children need a voice in the legal system. Of all my life experiences, this type of volunteer work resonated the most to me, as I have children of my own. And as a mother and survivor of a potentially deadly/abusive marriage, I unfortunately understand what it means for children to end up in environments that endanger and jeopardize their future. I joined the military to protect my children from the dangers of going into a social system due to the domestic violence within our home that was inflicted by the hands of their father. I was scared that if I did not join the military, their father would have ended up killing me, and my children would have ended up in the foster care system. There were times in which I thought I was not going to make it to see my sons grow up; times where I found myself praying before I would hear the click of a gun at my temple as my husband played Russian Roulette with my life.

I desire to use my law degree to assist families and children like Christian, and my own, in similar situations. My participation in this type of volunteer work is recent, but my aspirations to assist disenfranchised families is deep rooted. In the past, I have too often found myself lacking the requisite training to represent the disenfranchised and voiceless. It is for this reason I am applying to your law school. Because I am passionate about advocating for those who do not have a voice, I seek to acquire the necessary training to effectively be a voice for them. I would relish the opportunity to learn from experienced professors and to be able to apply their teachings towards my legal career. With their guidance, I hope to give my all to make a difference in the lives of young adults similar to Christian and others I have known.

Sample Eleven: Future Criminal Defense Attorney

I understand the importance of defending those who can't defend themselves. At a young age when I was dealing with bullies, I chose to stay quiet and shrug it off. Not because I was not capable of defending myself but because I was uncomfortable speaking up. Determined to prove myself, I became more outspoken. I started to become vocal in defense of myself. Becoming independent, driven, and outspoken were never characteristics of mine at five, eleven, or thirteen years old. However, I worked hard to advocate and always challenge myself and others.

In college, I landed a summer internship with the Texas Department of Justice (TX DOJ) in the Division of Recidivism, Reduction, and Re-Entry (DR3). My daily tasks involved researching vocational programs and technical training for offenders upon release. My research was critical because I would express to my boss the high demand and greater need for one program rather than another. This position sparked my passion for advocacy. I knew my work was meaningful because once I attended the inaugural classes graduation at Five Keys Detention Center, one newly released offender described how beneficial the programs I advocated for were to him. Once I completed my internship with TX DOJ, I was brought on as a part time staffer. I was excited to continue my work with TX DOJ but I was not

124

aware I would be transferred to the Bureau of Firearms (BOF) as a Special Assistant.

The BOF contained several Reagan-loving, Pro- open carry, "closeted" conservatives. This position was challenging for me as my personal views differed heavily from the agents in the BOF. For example, special agents were not focused on barriers to re-entry or what's next for the newly released. Instead, their main goal was getting offenders off the streets and behind cells for lengthy sentences. Casual office conversation regarding Trump's amazing race or how the judge should have invoked a longer sentence would make me scream internally. The position was mentally draining and there were days I contemplated quitting. After a few conversations with friends and family, I knew I needed to stay. In order to remain true to my passion, I became vocal about my views with my supervisor. I knew the agents may have not agreed with my perspective or the amazing work I was doing in the DR3; however, I was proud of my ability   to discuss any open, pending, or closed cases with agents and my supervisor. I began asking agents to explain the charges with me and the possible trajectory of offenders. From there, I would voice my concerns and advocate for an alternate route if applicable. I may have not been able to change the decisions of many cases but, this questioning established the basis for a great argument. While the DR3 helped me advocate for offenders' rights, the BOF prepared me to make my case against those whose viewpoints differ from my own.

I continue to be an advocate for others as I currently serve as Deputy Political Coordinator for the nation's first political action committee dedicated to fully supporting Black women candidates that want to run for office. I also currently assist with an organization which aims to drastically transform the criminal justice system. Being able to work on this project thus far has been informative and I am ready to take this knowledge with me to law school. The Criminal Justice Clinic

125

at your institution closely aligns with the reformations I want to make in the system. From my current and past roles, I know the importance of advocating for wrongfully convicted Black men and women. However, in order for me to do so to the extent I desire, I need to be provided with the correct legal knowledge and advocacy techniques to create change surrounding racial bias in the criminal justice system. Your prestigious institution will be an essential part of this process to help me become a great agent of criminal defense.

Sample Twelve: Undecided Law Path

Not many children know what they want to do with their lives at a young age. Yet I did. By the age of ten, I had seen my mother be physically abused by my father, and had heard her share detailed accounts of the struggles that she faced in family court while dealing with the divorce and trying to enforce a subsequent child support ruling. I remember telling my mother to hire a lawyer. At the time, I did not even fully understand exactly what lawyers did; I simply knew that lawyers helped people in situations that were beyond their control. She responded, however, that as a single mother shouldering the responsibility of putting two young daughters through private school on her own, hiring an attorney was not financially viable at that time. It hadn't dawned on me that cost would be an issue when it came to obtaining legal representation to handle an issue such as this. It was at that time that I realized what I wanted to do with my life. I wanted to help people - like my mom - who couldn't afford legal assistance.

I went on to enroll in St. John's University with dreams of finally achieving the goal that I had set for myself years before. Life had other plans. After my first semester, I entered into a relationship that quickly turned sour, and the emotional abuse that I endured left me feeling unconfident, lost and confused about my life. My grades suffered severely, and I jumped from school to school, eventually deciding to drop out. I felt a powerful sense of failure, one that was almost too great to bear. I convinced myself that my dream of

126

becoming an attorney was no longer attainable and decided to work various jobs in retail—a field that seemed a bit more "realistic" at that time.

Years later, unsatisfied with my job and still wanting to obtain my undergraduate degree, I decided to enroll in school again. Assuming that a career in law was no longer an option, I decided to pursue fashion because it felt more attainable for someone with my retail sales background. However, after graduating and working as a Product Development Assistant for a fashion designer in New York, I still found myself feeling unfulfilled and uninspired. I reached my breaking point one day while training a new hire. She excitedly asked me what I loved most about the job and the industry overall. I was speechless; I could not think of a single thing that I enjoyed. It was then that the truth hit me—I was miserable. I didn't enjoy my job and I didn't feel fulfilled. That night, I went home and cried for hours. I reflected on how I had become my own worst enemy and denied myself the opportunity to pursue my passion. I had written myself off out of fear that I was not good enough. I decided to turn my life around and pursue my original passion—a career in law.

For the first time in years, I no longer felt hopeless. I enrolled in St. John's paralegal program and attended classes during the evenings and weekends. I found myself feeling a renewed sense of purpose. Even after working full days as a fashion designer, I couldn't wait to attend class. Upon receiving my certification, I joined the civil rights law firm of Anderson & Anderson as a Legal Assistant and my time there has been life changing. Through my work with Anderson & Anderson, I've been able to speak with clients who are dealing with all sorts of trauma and I have not only witnessed, but also helped them receive justice for the harms that they've endured. In my time at the firm, I have worked with people feeling their most powerless – victims of police misconduct, sexual harassment, and discrimination. I have treasured the opportunity to play a part in vindicating their rights.

There is a need for dedicated people on the front lines to fight for what is right. My work experience has taught me attention to detail, critical thinking, and analytical skills that are necessary for success in the legal profession, and my time with Anderson & Anderson has reignited my passion for helping people who are vulnerable. After a long period of doubting myself, I've never been more sure that my purpose is to advocate for those who are unable to advocate for themselves. I am grateful for the life lessons garnered from my past mistakes. Not only have they strengthened my sense of certainty and purpose, they have also helped me to see just how much inner strength I possess. Only by losing my way was I able to get to where I am today—clear-eyed and full of resolve, ready to be a voice for the voiceless.

Sample Thirteen: Undecided Law Path

On June 29, 2006, I was prepared to become a big sister, but I never could have imagined that I would be taking on the role of a mother. The phrase "It's A Boy" did not mean nearly as much to me when I thought I would only be his sibling. At the time, I was {insert age} years old, and the youngest. I knew that a younger brother would mean my obligations in the household would increase, but I had no idea what was to come. Soon after my baby brother entered the world, I experienced a division in my family that would drastically change my life. My parents separated and my older brother went to live with my father without considering how this would impact our family. To keep us from homelessness, my mother worked constantly, which forced me into uncomfortable situations such as assuming the role of a mother.

My adolescence was interrupted, and adulthood quickly followed as the years went on. Instead of thinking about school dances and hanging out with friends, I was tasked with helping to raise a little boy. While maneuvering through school, learning the curriculum of my Advanced Placement courses, I became an expert at multitasking. After coming home from Beta Club and Tennis Practice I was also responsible for cooking, cleaning, and preparing him for bed, which oftentimes left me with little to no rest. As he got older, my life became more challenging because I was also tasked with being an educator. As

I studied for my own tests, I assisted him with his homework and taught him everything I could.

I was the product of a broken home, which meant taking care of my brother and also witnessing child support battles, divorce court, mediations, and lawyers. I remember hearing conversations about the courts forcing my father to give my mother money, along with discussions about my mother having sole custody. This life-changing experience ultimately sparked my interest in learning the law and becoming a lawyer.

This experience also taught me discipline and the true meaning of hard work. I figured out rather quickly that procrastination could not exist in my world if I wanted to succeed and become a lawyer. I majored in Criminal Justice so that I could take classes about the law, courts, prison system, and criminal procedures. These courses fueled my passion to be an advocate for others, especially for the underrepresented. I became comfortable with being uncomfortable in intimidating situations such as presenting for a class or speaking up about something I believed in. My life experiences strengthened my adaptability and flexibility in managing change.

Although I faced much adversity in my life, I persevered and became the first person in my family to graduate from college and to obtain a Master's Degree. I am thankful because my experiences have shaped me into a person who is ready to enter law school. The challenges I endured at a young age have given me valuable experience in balancing school with other responsibilities and extracurricular activities. I understand the importance of persistence when faced with adversity, challenging courses, and inconvenient situations. I am positive that by being conscientious and focused, law school will ultimately become another stepping stone that I will overcome.

Sample Fourteen: Future Human Rights Attorney

Tension and fear left me as I finally embraced the cold, yellowed face of my best friend Maribella at the airport. Acting as though I had calculated this very moment in my mind many times before, I led her to my car, watching out for anyone who threatened to take this freedom from her. She carefully snuck into the backseat of my car. Fragile, humbled, and fatigued, she embodied the long, tenuous escape from domestic slavery in Saudi Arabia. We drove home—our named destination of freedom. My mother's eyes of relief fastidiously rushed us into the house. Perhaps she sensed an impending danger we had not. Believing we had welcomed Maribella into a promised land of opportunity, my father and I excitedly offered Maribella water and food. She accepted water. A single tear sat in my father's lower eyelid as he carefully placed a glass of water into Maribella's skeletal fingers.

At this intersection of freedom, Maribella and I rested. Maribella had endured four days of travel through the Middle East and Europe to the United States with an expired American Passport. I had endured days of tireless supplication for help from the US Embassy, Customs, and a never-ending list of agencies. None were equipped to handle the improvised extensions of calculated decisions we had made over the past year.

In 2006, Maribella's family, our close family friends, moved to Saudi Arabia. Maribella was in the middle of completing her high school degree. Her family allowed her to stay with her aunt to complete her education. When she completed high school, she enrolled at a local university. That summer, Maribella was told that her mother had fallen ill and needed her care. We all cared deeply for her mother and saw her off. Because I often spent time at her aunt's house, Maribella asked me to keep her updated about the mail her aunt received regarding her college classes and financial aid. I did just that for a month.

My stomach sank when I received a chilling email in early 2009. Maribella wrote that her mother was not ill. She described the cold, tactful methods her mother and aunt had employed to get her to Saudi Arabia and use her as a domestic slave. For over a year, we covertly exchanged emails, planning the details of her escape. Our plans were plans calculated without interruption—the strongest and most volatile factor. Our plans were interrupted when her father announced that he had arranged her marriage to a man Maribella knew as cold, abusive, and elderly. She and I both knew that the transfer of ownership could occur within 24 hours.

130

Using the money I had saved from doing odd jobs for my neighbors and babysitting, I bought an airplane ticket. This purchase was the easiest task with the littlest amount of promise. Maribella was a young woman with an expired passport. There were few times at which she was not vigilantly supervised, and our supplications for help to the U.S. Embassy were lethargically answered. At sixteen years old, I placed trust in myself to construct a plan. Waiting for the "timely" response of the government was no longer a viable option. I was met with the unexpurgated task of helping my best friend navigate through the unknown to a place of safety. For days, I made extensive calls to any phone number of any governmental and airport agency I could get my hands on. It was clear that the art of life is not the act of overcoming but the act of improvising to overcome.

Improvising to overcome became essential to Maribella and my survival as her family in the US and Saudi Arabia began to question her whereabouts. I shyly pretended to know nothing of her disappearance. This act kept them convinced for the few days that Maribella travelled and arrived at my home. They sought elsewhere and everywhere to find and recapture this piece of currency they had just lost.

Meanwhile, Maribella and I rested in each other's presence, existing in a dangerous oblivion. Interruption delivered reality to our tired, fearful doorstep.

"Escondete! Escondete! Escondete!" I had never heard such tremor in my father's voice. And the words rung, standing bare—the only words that would come out of my father's mouth. Maribella didn't understand the words, but she knew as well as I knew that they meant "hide." Twenty seconds turned into an eternity as we scattered around the house one last time hiding any trails of Maribella's forbidden presence. Quickly, scrambling, we both squeezed into my brother's closet. Pressed to Maribella's shivering body, I never thought I would find comfort in a closet filled with the dusky scent of my brother's worn-out jerseys.

I found myself idle gripping onto a broken baseball bat. The silence allowed us to hear clearly the roaring motor of the familiar green van that had just pulled into my driveway. I could hear the shuffling and the whispers taking place behind our kind green door. The footsteps, the voices echoed in my mind. Over and over I could hear the low tones of the doorbell. Chaos quickly turned into an illusion of serenity. Evil was never static, and this became clear when it stepped into my house. The very people—our old friends, her aunt—who had sent Maribella away to imprisonment lamented her actions not because Maribella was a missing young adult, but because she had taken family gold from them. Calmly, my parents, feigning ignorance of what had occurred the past few days, welcomed them.

They left, suspicious and unconvinced. Only our refined sense of improvisation could guide us all to a semblance of safety. Soon enough, Maribella's family was able to trace the purchaser of the ticket. I received death threats and was followed for months. Thankfully, I had already arranged for Maribella's travel to our out of state relatives. Today, Maribella has a bachelor of science and is pursuing dentistry school.

Today, I am pursuing a Juris Doctor. I intend to become an advocate of human rights and civil liberties in international law working to bring equitable, sustainable contracts and treatises between enterprises, communities, and countries. I will likely never experience what my clients live in their communities. However, I will unwaveringly stand beside them and advocate for them, elevating their voices. I will approach the law knowing that it follows a plan that is often interrupted. But, I will navigate the law knowing that improvisation of that interrupted plan can save a life. These experiences have inculcated in me an unforgettable and unrelenting desire to practice a law that maintains human rights as a human necessity.

Sample Fifteen: Future Prosecutor

In my experience, the public tends to view the legal system as centered on the punishment of people who commit crimes. To me, the legal system is far from that. I believe it is a place where individuals who commit crimes have a place to right their wrongs and learn from that experience to become better members of their community. When I was offered an internship at a District Attorney's office, I was ecstatic.

I would finally get the chance to witness how this phenomenon works. Upon meeting the attorneys in the office, I was able to speak with an attorney who specialized in treatment courts. I was immediately intrigued because the purpose of treatment courts resonates very closely with the rehabilitative model of criminal justice that I believe in. She noticed my interest and invited me to attend a series of meetings and court proceedings with her.

The first meeting that I attended was a general meeting for the attorneys, mentors, treatment staff, and a judge. During this meeting, the status of various clients was discussed, how they have been responding to their treatment, and any changes to their treatment that may need to be made. At the conclusion of the meeting, there was a court session scheduled to share what was discussed in this meeting with the clients themselves. Immediately before this session began, to my surprise, the judge asked me to introduce myself to the group and what my interest was in treatment courts. I explained my personal view of the criminal justice system, and my desire to help people instead of punishing them. He assured me that was the goal of the alternative court system. He also told me that if this is what I am looking for, that I was in the right place and that I belonged here.

The court session that followed made me realize the truth in the judge's words. Client by client, their progress in the program was examined. I was able to witness people at every stage of the program. Having the side-by-side comparison of clients in multiple stages of their treatment was like night and day; the internal struggle with mental illness and addiction in the new clients was juxtaposed with the newly found lease on life that others demonstrated after having their issues addressed was astonishing. Although as an intern I did not have a direct hand in improving the quality of life of these clients, I will never forget the second-hand feeling of accomplishment, and something I will always strive to achieve.

I strongly believe that when we reimagine the idea of a punitive justice system into one that focuses on rehabilitation, the individuals who are within the system benefit. Too often, after an individual spends time in prison for their crimes, they are released with no job, housing, money, or emotional support. These are all things that are necessary to thrive; without these items, failure and a relapse of criminal behavior is almost guaranteed. However, I've witnessed how when these individuals are given the support they need (as seen in the treatment courts), they now have all the tools necessary to restart their life on the right foot, and are less likely to commit crimes in order to obtain what they need to survive. Simply put, when individuals are provided with the help they need, criminal behavior becomes less of a   survival tactic. I know of individuals who were once homeless and stealing food and other necessities to survive that are now contributing members of society, which fares better for all members of the community.

I have always been the one to lend a helping hand - whether it be service events, homework, or even personal advice – and I wish to continue to help others succeed. This internship experience was pivotal and solidified my decision to become an attorney. In a world where punishment is often the first reaction, there needs to be more people who are interested in redemption and looking out for the greatest good for the accused individual, as well as supporting others when they need it the most. That's the kind of attorney that I aim to become.

Sample Sixteen: Future Immigration Law Attorney

I have been writing poetry since the age of seven, exactly three months after I arrived to the United States with nothing but a pink backpack around my shoulders and my mother's grip around my left hand. My mother kept us in Mexico for as long she could to root me in all things Tijuana. Finally, when she turned 23 and sensed our last opportunity for change, we said goodbye to *mi abuelita, mi tio Fernando,* the *panaderia* down the street, and we left to America. I remember hugging my mother's leg and peering up at her as she surrendered our passports to the men in army green at the Tijuana, Baja California border. I wondered if she was sad like me—her face so still. Her eyes glazed, movements calculated down to her breath. My mother brought me to this country to fulfill my purpose, sacrificing her motherland and trading *bunuellos* for American apple pie that tasted sour on her tongue.

134

The culture shock I endured upon arriving to the United States, foreign to the English language, caused me to retreat to automatic assimilation. My mother and I shared my auntie's garage in Chula Vista. We didn't have to heat our water on the stove anymore to bathe, and due to WIC, we always had gallons of milk and canned vegetables. I felt fortunate, yet fearful, that any misbehavior would illustrate that I didn't deserve to be in the U.S. Thus, I kept my Hispanic, immigrant background hidden. Still, every night, I could see the longing of Mexico in my mother's worried eyes. At a very young age, curled next to her on our air mattress, I decided that our trip to America would not be in vain.

It took more than a decade to properly digest the narrative that I once concealed, that intertwined with hardships and adversities, molds the story that I now acknowledge as my own. My mother works as a hotel maid, and nights when she clocked out of 10-hour shifts, she would come home and take off her shoes, bone tired from cleaning. Her feet were bruised and stung with arthritis. Through a stream of tears, she crawled into bed with me and whispered, "This right here *chikis,* this is why you need to stay in school. This is for you." When there was a drive-by shooting at our house and we needed to move, my mother found a way. Making something out of nothing, she rescued us from homelessness and lifted me from the hands of institutionalization. Certainly, there are moments that my mother wishes to leave in the past, like when I would wait for her in the car while she danced at a local strip club in Las Vegas to make ends meet, or when she would hold me close during nights when we would sleep in her '93 Jeep Cherokee in Mexico. However, instead, I have internalized those moments, and realized that they serve as a testament to how far my future can reach. In her book, *Becoming*, Michelle Obama states, "Even when it's not pretty or perfect. Even when it's more real than you want it to be. Your story is what you have, what you will always have. It is something to own."

By the time I began middle school, my household existed on the poverty line, in an underdeveloped neighborhood in North Las Vegas, where I was quickly introduced to the American criminal justice system. My stepfather and mother had both been incarcerated on separate accounts. My mother was persuaded to plead "Guilty" for a crime she did not commit in exchange for a lighter sentence; the defense attorney relayed to my mother that as a young black woman with broken English in front of a jury, her lamentable faith was inevitable. On both occasions that I saw my parents in hand cuffs, I felt powerless. I still taste the warm, flat apple juice my school counselor gave me as I waited for a police officer to enter the room and tell me that my mother—my lifeline in America—was in a jail cell. I felt small and invisible and convinced, more than ever, that this country did not want me. But it was in my ability to sit at the police station, crisscrossed, writing lines of poetry in a yellow notepad, that I found a sense of being. I was my mother's daughter, I could read, and I could write—surely I was someone.

It is this culmination of experiences that I have assumed as an Afro-latina immigrant in the United States that allows me to state, with conviction, that when you grow up poor, brown, and female in America, you are looking for power—for me, it is power to help others with stories that reflect mine. When I entered the legal field in New York City, the value of narration stretched beyond my personal anecdote. There was a reason why my client Marisol was in this country undocumented; her husband brought her to America, abused her, and left her on the street without legal residency. The two years of deferment that I took before entering law school to serve underprivileged communities merely heightened my interest in not only law, but public service and immigration reform. From providing legal services to undocumented women suffering from sexual abuse and domestic violence at a non-profit organization, to undertaking political asylum pro bono cases at Sidley Austin LLP, a mere inclination towards the legal field quickly transformed itself into my purpose in America.

Sample Seventeen: Future Civil Rights Attorney

It was early in June of 2020, several days after George Floyd had been killed while in the custody of police. I was thousands of miles away from Minnesota but little did I know I would feel the impact of what had occurred. I remember stopping at the intersection, the light was red; I could hear the protestors yelling chants. "Black Lives Matter!", "Say their names!" Before I knew it my patrol car was completely surrounded by protestors. At that moment I was unsure what would happen next; but I knew it would be a life changing moment. While surrounding my patrol vehicle, some of the black protesters began to yell "Which side are you on friend? Which side are you on?" At that moment, as I reflected on my life, I couldn't help but wonder "how exactly, did I end up here?" I felt as if the black community and law enforcement were at war; this put me at war with myself.

In that moment, however, I was seen only as someone who represented a system that has killed and oppressed people who look just like me. I wished in that moment to be able to explain to the protestors that we had the same goal and possibly similar backgrounds, but I had taken a different route to bring about systemic change.

I did not grow up like most of my coworkers whom I would stand beside with tactical gear on during the protests to come. While growing up in a small rural town, I noticed there were incidents where systemic and individual violations of the law would often go unchecked. Many of my friends and family witnessed and experienced racial discrimination from an early age. My father is a convicted felon and would go on to miss significant moments in my life due to an unlawful arrest. I vowed that I would one day learn how to shape or change laws that unfairly harm historically oppressed communities.

Becoming a lawyer had always been a goal of mine since I could remember. However, the semester before graduating I decided I was not mentally or financially ready to attend law school. With law school on hold for a few years I decided I would pursue a career in law enforcement.

For the past four and a half years I have been a police officer. I had originally begun my career in law enforcement to bridge the gap between the African American community and law enforcement. Little did I know, as I would make small and large strides to bridge the gap, there would be things out of my control that would drive a wedge between law enforcement and African American communities everywhere. I would be left time after time feeling inadequate, as if my hard work and dedication was in vain. This was due to the fact that I was unable to bring about systemic changes.

While I have decided to trade in my badge and pursue my law degree, my goal remains the same; I plan to bring about systemic changes as a civil rights attorney and my journey begins with law school. I look forward to the opportunity to take the next step in my career and to study law under the direction of the school's dedicated faculty and staff.

Sample Eighteen: Future Juvenile Justice Attorney

When I was six years old, before my mother passed away, she decided to have my grandmother raise me. Her decision was made out of love, courage, and desperation – it was the "right" thing for her to do because as a mother, you want to do what is best for your child and it wasn't best to leave my care in the hands of my abusive father. However, because my father was still my custodial parent, my time was split between my grandmother's home in Harlem and my father's home in Brooklyn. Although I lived in two different houses, I never truly had a home and had no idea what that level of permanency could feel like until I entered the courtroom.

For the next eleven years, my childhood embodied trauma. Every week, I shuffled back and forth on the subway, between school, my grandmother's, and my father's house. My father was an alpha male who always wanted to assert his authority and power. He liked to be in control, especially when he felt wrong. This is why, despite having a college degree, he stuck to jobs in correctional facilities like Rikers Island and juvenile detention centers. Although he was proud of me, my father always wanted to break me down. By the time I was seventeen, I had sustained eleven years of physical, mental, and verbal abuse in his house. When I look back, I don't see a home or safety.

My father overdosed on crack cocaine and methadone the day before New Year's Eve in 2016. His addiction was hard on us all. It squeezed every bit of love and life out of our relationship, but he was

138

still my father. We were both held hostage by his addiction and the hostile environment it created, but I can now say that we're both finally free.

Not long after my father's death, I started my current job representing the New York City Department of Education at impartial hearings involving students with learning challenges. When I began my job more than three years ago, I experienced an adrenaline rush each time I prepared for hearings that impacted children in need of assistance. Over time, my job gave me confidence because I had a voice and could be heard as an advocate. State-appointed hearing officers knew me and listened to me. After three years, I now feel like a fixture in these hearing rooms. These rooms make me feel like I am finally home.

I often think about what drew me to this education work. Initially, I did not realize that I saw myself in my cases. I had never been treated as a child in need of assistance (even though I was). I am helping students just like me – the ones that have been silenced and are not allowed to speak up for fear of retaliation and punishment. Today, having a voice in the courtroom does not make up for the pain, drug abuse, dark nights, and silence of my upbringing. But it does allow me to help children from broken homes where abuse is accepted due to ignorance or repeatedly being mistaken for tough love. A career in Juvenile and Restorative Justice will allow me to use mediation and other legal skills to help young people reconcile differences. I want to continue to be a voice for juveniles who have been abused, neglected, and abandoned by a system that has failed them. I want them to see that I am just like them and I am not going to fail them. I am going to do whatever I can to make sure they get the justice they deserve.

My story is one of survival, resilience, grit, triumph, and most of all freedom. Freedom to choose my own path despite the cards that life dealt me. I learned a long time ago that I do not need to be ashamed of what I couldn't control, and I can accomplish anything despite the hand I was dealt. No challenge, including law school, is too big to face when I've already overcome so much. Attending Seton Hall University School of Law does not feel like a choice, but rather a need. I need to pursue a deeper legal education to further my career as a juvenile advocate. Your clinical offerings in social and juvenile justice will allow me to deepen my understanding of the laws affecting our education system and economies and give me the opportunity to turn my passion into a legal career.

Sample Nineteen: Future Criminal Defense Attorney

They forced my arms back and put me in handcuffs. The room was spinning and I was numb to the core. I was confused, tired, cold, and scared. The men in black armored suits took me outside into the freezing January morning and threw me chest first onto the cold, wet grass. Through my tear-filled eyes I managed to see the men in black taking my father away with them, on their backs read the letters "DEA".

I was nine years old when my father sat me down and explained to me that most of my extended family was part of a drug trafficking ring that had been operating for over five years now. I was in complete and utter shock. The years sped by and it wasn't until January 25, 2012, when I was sixteen that that unforgettable night occurred. My family and I were staying over at an uncle's house because our home was inhabitable for a couple of days. It was three in the morning when the front and back door were knocked down, the men in black and armored suits were yelling for everyone to get out of the rooms and put their arms up. It all happened so fast, fear turned to tears as one of the men put all the adults, including me, in handcuffs. I was thrown on the front lawn chest first only to look up and see my father taken away. Before I knew it, the early morning was everywhere I looked; "Kirkland man among 20 busted by DEA for drug trafficking" (The Kirkland Reporter), "20 arrested during drug raids in Seattle and Bay Area" (The Seattle Times).

Growing up my parents couldn't afford to pay a sitter to watch me while they were at work so I spent the weekends and summer days watching all the Court TV my tired little eyes could handle. I was obsessed with it all; the drama, the litigation, opening and closing statements, cross examination, etc. I would watch all the reruns and never get tired of them. It was during the "Jenny Jones Trials" rerun when Geoffrey N. Fieger was cross examining that I told myself "that's going to be me." Never in a million years did I think I'd be on the other side of the TV screen. After

140

my father was taken away by the DEA agents, my mother and I had to figure out how to get him out because his only crime was being in the wrong place at the wrong time. My father ended up getting caught in the mess of it all; court dates, public defender disputes, plea bargains, etc. Neither of my parents spoke English well and the fact that my father's public defender didn't either, wasn't helpful. We ended up hiring a defense attorney to help my father out; not only was it expensive, but the communication was terrible. Neither of my parents speak or understand English well so my whole life it's been up to me to be their personal interpreter. From the DMV, to calling the cable company, to opening a home loan. This wasn't any different. There were times when I skipped entire school days because my father had a court date or there was a meeting with the defense attorney, and I needed to be there as a backup interpreter. The attorney had hired a translator for us but it cost thousands more and having to communicate through a third party was extremely uncomfortable.

After three years, my father was finally released. After all the tears, the stress, and the money spent, I was able to hug my dad once again. If the experience of my dad being falsely accused and then found not guilty taught me anything it is that I am destined to be a defense attorney myself. Being trilingual gives me the chance to be my own interpreter for the people; I don't want others to go through what I went through. As a Latina woman who grew up in a lower-middle class household I know what it's like to be treated as a minority; when it comes to exonerations Hispanics are vastly underrepresented. The number of white and African American inmates exonerated for false convictions matches or exceeds their percentage of the inmates in prison. Meanwhile, Hispanic exonerees only account for twelve percent, despite making up twenty-two percent of the prison population. And only four percent of lawyers are Hispanic; I strongly believe that the lack of adequate legal representation is partly due to a lack of culturally competent lawyers. Language alone can become a huge barrier for the defendants even if there is an interpreter. You have to take a lot into account, for example: was the interpreter qualified? How do we know what was said when the transcript is not available in Spanish? How can we be so sure that what the client said was translated correctly and whether they understood their rights one hundred percent? The last thing needed is to seem like the client is trying to cover up information when it's a translation issue. My Hispanic roots and my fluent Spanish (and French) will allow me to directly communicate with many clients without having to worry about a third-party interpreter. I see how underrepresented the Latinx community is and I want to be part of the change. My own experience with the legal system has only given me the motivation to be part of that change and to become a lawyer.

Sample Twenty: Future Civil Rights Attorney

The first racial disparity incident I was able to fully understand was the case of an unarmed, 17-year-old Trayvon Martin. Knowing that a young, black teenager lost his life because he "looked suspicious" while walking home from purchasing skittles and juice was, and still is puzzling. It left an uneasy feeling in my stomach. Martin's murderer, George Zimmerman, would be later found not guilty of the malicious crime. Zimmerman was acquitted of all charges filed against him after claiming self-defense against a minor who had no weapon nor showed any signs of criminal activity. To add insult to injury, Zimmerman would later start autographing skittle bags for fun. When the criminal justice system failed Trayvon, I felt as if it failed me as well. Whatever hope I had that racial discrimination no longer existed faded away instantly. The world suddenly seemed to become this evil place where the law proved to be different for different races.

The multitude of similar cases that followed, struck a feeling I can't seem to bear. Staring at the T.V. screen; watching newsclip after newsclip of all of the unthinkable tragedies affecting my people due to racial disparities, followed by injustices, has been heartbreaking. As the tears fell after learning of each misfortune and my body began to grow cold, I became more angry, more afraid, yet more determined. Angry for my people. Afraid for my people. Determined to help my people.

Racial discrimination with the inclusion of police brutality have been carried over into today's society from before slavery with little to no action from the criminal justice system to cease it. I am brave enough to willingly fight for the rights of racial minorities by stepping forward to challenge the system we abide by yet that fails us repeatedly.

142

Black men are rushed with guns sometimes resulting in death for stealing out of a convenience store, yet white men who massacre schools often live to see their punishment without harm. This is America. The same America that is in need of change.

Emphasizing that movements such as "Black Lives Matter" isn't just a trend, but a commitment to justice and a cry for help is imperative. This is a nation where all citizens are supposed to be granted "equal protection under the law" and yet this is the same nation where seemingly more Blacks face more hardships and unfairness within the system than Whites. Helping clients fight through a justice system that seems to be unjust is my goal.

Although giving equality to everyone should not be debatable, there are closed-minded people who detest those that are fighting for rights that were earned decades ago, or so we thought. For example, former President Trump stood by silently when peaceful protesters were met with smoke bombs and guns by law enforcement and troops. In response to the unjust killings of George Floyd, Ahmaud Arbery, Breonna Taylor, and many others, protesters were marching when they were attacked, and even arrested. Meanwhile, after Trump supporters forced their way into the Capitol, their reception and consequences were very different. It is these realities that trigger me, leading me to know I am destined to become a civil rights attorney to guide and protect the minority community. I would love nothing less than for your law school to help me fulfill that calling.

Sample Twenty-One: Future Criminal Defense Attorney

It was that time again. Students were asked to stand up and introduce themselves to the classroom. I cleared my throat, stood tall and began introducing myself while following the prompts on the board. "Hello everyone, my name is Kiara. I'm a 29-year-old single mother taking five classes and working two jobs." My excitement to meet my new classmates became overrun by the surprised faces in the crowd. After class introductions I was often met by professors advising me that their class is demanding and that my stringent scheduled may not be compatible. I always assured my professors that my hard work and positive outlook would allow me to complete my degree as I have always planned. I have now completed my degree with a cumulative GPA of 3.6 – something they did not believe I would do.

Growing up in a two-parent household, I would have never imagined becoming a single parent. I expected to marry young, start a family, and become a lawyer by thirty. Nevertheless, at the age of 22, I decided to continue my education by obtaining my bachelor's degree. At the age of 24, I discovered that my son was not developing as well as his peers. That same year, my son was diagnosed with autism spectrum disorder. Balancing school, working 63 hours a week and being a parent was beyond difficult, but it demonstrated my willpower.

As a parent to a child on the spectrum, my goals are like any other parent's. I desire to raise my child to become a fully functional adult that can take care of themselves and make a positive contribution to society. One of the most challenging parts of being a parent to a child on the spectrum is navigating the legalities of parental rights and witnessing the lack of sufficient advocacy available for my child. For example, school district are known to discriminate and transfer students on the spectrum instead of providing the appropriate training for teachers and staff. Removing children with disabilities from school districts does not solve problems. Training and additional resources to handle such students is what enables schools to overcome their challenges. At one point, *my* child's school district wanted to remove him instead of training their staff. After only 50 days of my son attending their school district, they wanted him out. When I learned of this, I was against the school district moving my son to another school district just because they refused to educate themselves. Thus, once the school requested a private placement I refused. I filed a hearing request letter with the superintendent within 10 days of my objection to the school district's proposal. Ultimately, the voices of my child and I were heard. My hearing request was granted, and I was promised an opportunity to allow my son to remain in the school district. In addition, a specialist was assigned to train the teachers and staff on how to work with students on the spectrum.

My personal adversity led my interest in advocating for the wrongfully accused. It also led to my interest in pursuing a career in disability rights. Raising a child with a disability is already challenging. I believe that too often parents and children are denied their rights simply because they don't know what their rights are or because they don't know how to properly advocate for themselves and their child like I had to. As a lawyer and advocate, I hope to be a resource to similarly situated parents – someone that helps them navigate systems and get the resources that they and their child deserve. Despite the boxes that others may try to put me in, or the low expectations that past professor have initially held for me, I am a determined, hardworking, and ambitious woman, capable of fulfilling any goals that I strive for. My past is a testament to my refusal to allow circumstances to predict my future. I believe that overcoming my personal hardships serves as evidence that I can succeed as a law student.

Sample Twenty-Two: Future Public Interest Attorney

The first time I saw a gun was when my father placed one to my mother's head, threatening to kill her. Desperate for an escape, my mother and grandparents hired a coyote - an individual who is paid to get people across the border - to get us away from my abusive father. A month later, my mother and I, along with my siblings, left all we had known in Mexico to come to the United States. At seven years old, from the trunk of the car, I saw a coyote drive my two younger brothers and myself illegally across the Texas border into the United States. I remember armed forces searching her car as we lay still in the trunk. Minutes later we were in the United States. We stopped at a nearby store and came out wearing Pokémon Pikachu shirts so we could blend in. This simple act of crossing a border has made me an undocumented, first-generation American and student, an identity that has come to shape my life experiences and opportunities.

Despite the difficulties these identities have placed on me, I never questioned my mother's decision to flee Mexico; my life in the United States has given me the opportunity to advocate for my family, assist attorneys with Deferred Action for Childhood Arrivals program, and assist victims of consumer fraud. Throughout these experiences, I have seen the critical need for lawyers that come from my community and believe that obtaining a Juris Doctor will grant me the knowledge and ability to continue to uplift and serve marginalized populations, such as my own.

When I began considering college, I realized I was ineligible to attend because of my legal status. In 2012, President Obama announced Dream Act and later Deferred Action for Childhood Arrivals (DACA), providing me a pathway to go to school. With the help of Dream Act, I was able to attend Reedley College where I began working with the Education and Leadership Foundation to promote awareness towards the Dream Act. Here, I volunteered to work with immigration attorneys to help applicants with DACA and assisted with their application filings. The center was continuously over occupancy for the first few months. I remember applicants being worried that they were at risk of deportation. Through this process, I became intimately aware of the anxiety that came with being undocumented among others in my community. I witnessed just how fragile this balance was, and the overwhelming fear that comes with this uncertainty. I was able to relieve that uncertainty for numerous people by helping them apply for DACA, something that I myself do every two years. This experience reaffirmed to me the privilege that comes with obtaining a higher education, a privilege that should not depend on citizenship status. This advocacy role allowed me to have a tangible impact in assisting others and was a skill that I came to use when my own family became victims of consumer fraud.

In 2015, my family became the victim of "Solar Panel Scams" that tied a lien to our house to the order of $90,000. This was the result of a solar company forging my mother's signature on a contract. Families like mine were told the solar panels were free but were later mailed a forged contract that tied liens to their property if the solar

146

panels were not paid off. Upon learning of this situation, I filed a complaint with the Texas State Contractors License Board to begin a legal investigation. The investigation led me to be in direct contact with the fraudulent company's legal counsel. Through months of back and forth, they provided my family with a settlement to cancel the solar contract, full ownership of the $90,000 solar system, and compensation for all property damages. Soon after this experience, I found that my family was not the only one targeted by this solar panel scheme.

After learning that this was a perpetual trend in 2015, I worked to help other families that were vulnerable to this illegal activity by founding the Solar Fraud Project. The Solar Fraud Project analyzes contracts, prepares complaint files to initiate legal investigations, and communicates with all parties from start to finish to provide families with settlements and property repairs. In order to help families in need, I provide pro-bono services and tailor each unique case to provide the Texas State Contractors License Board with as much evidence as possible. So far, I have helped coordinate and win eight cases on my own, not only getting liens off of the homes and canceling $540,000 in solar contracts, but also having the families receive settlements and property repairs. In 2017, I partnered with the Central Texas Legal Services to provide free legal aid to families in need to resolve additional cases through legal proceedings. I currently assist families facing bankruptcy and other fraudulent activities with Solar companies across Texas, and I continue to see the need for lawyers from my own community. Without the critical thinking and analytical skills a Juris Doctor offers, the work I can do for these families is limited. Coupled with a Juris Doctor degree, I can become a stronger, more effective advocate for underrepresented communities.

Nineteen years ago, I illegally crossed the border to start a new life away from my abusive father. My close proximity to the law, something that many in my community fear, has allowed me to see the vast power an understanding of the law can bring. My advocacy that once started with my mom has led me to a journey helping DACA recipients and victims of consumer fraud. Through these experiences, I have witnessed how the law can protect vulnerable populations and I believe that I can continue to help protect the rights of those in my community. In this way, obtaining a Juris Doctor will allow myself—an individual once ineligible to have rights or an education—the opportunity to fight for the rights of others. An opportunity only possible for me in my country, the United States of America.

Sample Twenty-Three: Future Intellectual Property (IP Law) Attorney

In my second semester at NYU I took my first art history class. My professor opened the first day with a slide show and gave a little backstory for each piece: a ceramic bowl from China, a hand painted scroll from Japan, brass sculptures from India, water colors from Korea, etc. She told us that each of the pieces she'd shown was a part of the Metropolitan Museum of Art in New York City's private collection. She then ended the lecture with a question, "To what extent have colonialism and imperialism played a role in the art world and how we engage with art today?" With each of the following classes she explored the complexities of art, cultural artifacts, and the ethics of preservation.

A year later, I spent my summer interning in the curatorial department at the Studio Museum in Harlem. As an intern, I got to take a tour of their private collection. Some of the works dated all the way back to the 1600s and were made by Africans enslaved in the United States. The fact that these pieces were under the care of a Black museum in Harlem felt something like a tangible first step to answering my professor's question. As a Black American, the direct descendant of enslaved Africans, the opportunity to be in the presence of that kind of history felt insurmountable.

On the day of the tour, one of the curators walked us out of the museum and led us around the block. When we stopped at a commercial self-storage building, I was confused. How could *this* be the site where the private collection was stored? The collection was spread across a few floors, and on those floors there were artworks everywhere. It was beautiful, but something was off. This facility was nothing like the temperature and humidity controlled facility I thought we'd see. I remember the curator pointing out a specific work that had been a part

148

of a performance piece in the 70s that couldn't be shown anymore because heat was causing the glue that held the work together to come apart. There were oil paintings that had cracked and weathered in the frigid winters. I knew the Studio Museum was doing the best they could with the funds they had, but I was disappointed.

Earlier that summer on a tour of another museum's permanent collection storage facility, I'd learned that preservation guidelines can be worked into an artist's or a specific work's contract. Black art and Black artists have always existed, but it would be naive to think that the legacies of slavery, Jim Crow segregation, and systemic racism haven't played a role in the lack of agency afforded to Black artists and the preservation of Black cultural artifacts. I wondered how many of the works in the storage unit had contracts. I wondered about reparations and the systems in place that were preventing the Studio Museum from being able to afford proper storage facilities. I wondered about all the history and historical objects that had already been and would soon be forever lost. I thought back to my first art history course and the question my professor asked on the first day, "To what extent have colonialism and imperialism played a role in the art world and how we engage with art today?".

The art my professor showed us on that first day and the art in the Studio Museum's collection are similar in that they are both tangible remnants of the imperialist and racist history of art collecting. For a large part of the Studio Museum's collection, the artists creating were never afforded access to contracts, let alone conservation rights. For many Black artists, creating in a time where Black people were not thought of as full citizens stripped them of their autonomy as artists, their ability to protect their intellectual property, and the opportunity to control their own narrative. The night of my tour of the Studio Museum's private collection I stayed up until 2am researching the legalities of preservation and the possibility of retroactive contracts for artists who were making art in a time when Black artists weren't even seen as artists.

In my wildest dreams, beyond law school, I'm working as an intellectual property lawyer representing Black artists and content-creators past and present. Entering law school, I am eager to continue my pursuit of the answers to my art history professor's question. I'm confident the answer lies somewhere at the intersection of art law, intellectual property law, critical race theory, and reparations.

Sample Twenty-Four: Future Environmental Law Attorney

"Girl, you want to drink from *that*?"

Misti held her hair away from her face and bent down to drink from an oddly rusted water fountain at our university campus. She stepped away from the fountain and looked at me with dismay and disgust, unable to believe what she had almost drank from. She stood quiet with shock for a few seconds. Meanwhile, I questioned my loyalty to my school—I could not believe that some parents were spending their entire life savings to send their children to a universally renowned institution that did not even facilitate good water quality for its students. The kick of adrenaline made my eyes shine; with my voice two tones higher than usual from the excitement, I said, "Let's test this water!"

During my second semester as a master's student studying environmental metrology and policy, my research group found abnormally high lead levels in some of the drinking water sources at Georgetown University's campus. Samples from The Office of Planning and Facilities Management and the fifth floor of White Gravenor Hall exceeded the EPA standard of 15 ppb or were very close to doing so. The Office of Planning and Facilities Management housed mostly African American and Latino workers, while the fifth floor of White Gravenor Hall was a lab used by a newly created department with limited funding. I strongly believed that such a specific lack of access to clean water was a form of environmental injustice, especially when dormitory water fountains were already equipped with filters. However, despite my belief that the school would jump to take action, they told me that exceeding the 15 ppb action level is not a legal violation and the school only needs to "perform certain required actions".

150

I was so confused; as a scientist, I could prove that the school was responsible for providing lead-contaminated water to staff but the school had no legal responsibility of the health consequences of giving such water. The experience opened my eyes to how a lack of education in one's environmental rights often disproportionately affects the voiceless minority populations and those who are undereducated about their rights. The lack of access to clean drinking water is often portrayed as an isolated issue in a different continent, or an anomaly that only occurs in poor cities like Flint, Michigan, but it was also happening right before my eyes. Clean drinking water should not be a privilege. The United Nations has even classified clean drinking water as a basic human right. The complicating terminology and vagueness of the school's representative piqued my interest in expanding my education to environmental law. I want to represent and fight for those, like the campus workers, who do not even know they have the right to access clean water. I want to educate people and let them know that access to clean air, water and land is a human right that must be uplifted by system actors and our government. I want to help those who have been negatively impacted by environmental hazards, but have been left alone in the dark to educate, solve, and pay themselves for problems that other companies have made.

I know your law school will be a perfect fit for me as the Environmental Law program shows me that the program shares my belief that an interdisciplinary view is needed with the application of the best available science to environmental lawmaking. From Hazardous Waste to Water Rights Law, the school's vast range of environmental courses to choose from excites me. The Program offers students such an amazing list of classes to choose from, taught by legal scholars and experts who are actively writing, working, and blazing the trail in these evolving legal fields. Furthermore, the Global Center for Environmental Legal Studies, the Energy & Climate Center, and Land Use Law Center will all allow me to gain environmental and community health case-practice while learning about the complex, interdisciplinary area of legal practice. I look forward to the chance of working with experts with the knowledge and resources to enrich and enable me to reach my potential and truly flourish.

Sample Twenty-Five: Future Civil Rights Attorney

I believe that I was born to be a civil rights attorney. Growing up in Birmingham, Alabama I was surrounded by the remnants of the Civil Rights Movement. I was adopted by my grandparents, who had strong beliefs about equality, and who in their lifetime supported many leaders who are recognized today, such as Angela Davis, Martin Luther King, and Malcolm X. To my family, these individuals were prominent people who created change by empowering others and challenging the legal system in the United States. As I grew, I became fascinated by many court cases, and by the implementation of the Civil Rights Act of 1964. I tried to make sense of these actions and the impact they made on my life as an African American. What does this mean for me? What responsibilities do I have to continue a legacy of social justice?

Despite having more opportunities because of the obstacles my ancestors faced, I recognize the obstacles that have challenged me. I was born in New York City and my life began in a sea of foster and kinship care situations. I was removed from my birth mother when I was two, after she attempted to protect herself from her abusive husband with a gun. Hazy memories of large courtrooms fill my earliest memories. Amidst the distorted images of my childhood, I distinctly remember my kindergarten graduation. Standing in an enormous auditorium filled with what seemed like the "whole world", I was tasked with the responsibility of stating what I wanted to be when I grew up. I anxiously spoke these words into the microphone: "My name is Jilisa Milton, and when I grow up I want to be a lawyer." Looking back, I am amazed at the level of self-awareness I had at that age.

I went to college as a first-generation student at the University of Alabama. Despite my childhood dreams, I began college as a nursing major, beginning the career my parents wanted for me. I soon realized the error in my judgment: I was taking classes that did not develop my strengths, and that I was not passionate about. My first years of college were difficult and confusing. I spent three years as a nursing student until I changed my major to social work and enrolled in Student Support Services, a program lending administrative support to first generation students. I had decided to follow my dream.

Many things have felt like concrete barriers. During college I worked in order to send money to my family, and dealt with the difficult news that my mother had been diagnosed with breast cancer. Social work became my crack in the concrete, my way of understanding how to be resourceful. Each semester, my grade point average increased, and I felt as though I had finally found my educational bearings. I began to look for outlets for my interests.

I became one of the founding members of the University of Alabama's chapter of Alabama ARISE Citizens Policy Project, an organization dedicated to promoting fair public policies for low income Alabamians. At this time, my eyes were open to laws that placed people from lower socioeconomic status at a disadvantage. The work I did in college inspired me to begin contemplating about what I should do after I finished my degree. Little did I know that a future law student was developing.

After college I joined AmeriCorps. I moved to Apopka, FL, a rural community with a rich culture in the midst of issues such as poverty, immigration reform, and education disparity. The Hope Community Center in Apopka serves as a beacon of hope for the immigrant community, and is the mother organization for the AmeriCorps program. My involvement in this program changed my life. I witnessed a part of a grassroots movement, and learned that undocumented immigrants faced adversities that I couldn't imagine. I served as the assistant to the Service Learning Coordinator, and watched as students from colleges around the country came to live with immigrants and learn about their experiences.

That year I was invited to a leadership conference in Chicago: Volunteers Exploring Vocation. During that time, I attended a breakout session that analyzed the words of professor at the Ohio State University and civil rights attorney Michelle Alexander. I was inspired by her book entitled "The New Jim Crow: Mass Incarceration at the

Age of Colorblindness". It presented research about how our prison system has ultimately created a permanent undercaste; a group of second-class citizens that are prevented from progressing in society. This undercast seemed to be excessively saturated with African American males, and affects the African American community on many levels. A passion grew for this movement, and I made the final decision to apply for law school.

I am currently in my second year as an AmeriCorps volunteer. I am a court advocate for Harbor House, a domestic violence agency in central Florida. I am able to learn more about the court process, as well as reflect about how domestic violence has made an impact on my own life. I am inspired by the families I assist every day, and I am able to combine my love for Social Work with my love of law on a daily basis. I assist petitioners with understanding the injunction process, and serve as a community resource for survivors of domestic, sexual, and dating violence. I challenge myself to speak to groups of people about domestic violence through my own experiences in the hopes to creating an effective a call to action.

I want to continue my education by enrolling in an MSW/JD dual enrollment program at an accredited university. I hope to grow as an activist, and as leader. Even though my understanding of the legal system, social justice, and my passion to serve others has grown exponentially since I stood on that stage as a five year old, my dream remains the same: "My name is Jilisa Milton, and I want to be a civil rights attorney".

Sample Twenty-Six Future Entertainment Law Attorney

When I was 5 years old, my mother enrolled me into my very first ballet classes at a tiny dance studio on Ventura Boulevard. Our first exercise was to create a dance where we embodied the personality of our favorite animal. For this, I chose my favorite animal - a lion. Upon stepping onto the dancefloor to perform for the class, however, I instantly felt the familiar manifestation of stage fright take over me. However, it was Ms. Marie's last statement before my performance that kept me on the dance floor. "Forget about your classmates watching you Jhanel," she called out from the corner of the room. "Become the lion and tell everyone your story!"

Once the music began, I internalized Ms. Marie's advice and suddenly it was all like magic. As I took on the movements and expressions of a lion, the story unraveled around me and I was no longer a scared little girl dancing in a classroom, but a lion in the jungle. My classmates watched both in awe and intimidation, anticipating my movements for the next part of my story. In that moment, I began to realize that the world of the arts was the perfect place where I could openly express myself through my creations, my movements, and through music. Ms. Marie showed me how storytelling in dance could be a place where I could loudly and freely express myself to my audience, without judgement or objections. When I danced, I had a voice and I could speak directly to those who were watching me so that they could see me, my message, and my thoughts. Where they could understand me. Over the years, dance became the art form that shaped me into the brave and outspoken individual I am today.

When I started working as an extra in television and films, I was exposed to dozens of entertainers without a voice of their own. As a single mother of twins, it was a challenge for my mother to financially support my sister and I. Because my sister and I were accustomed to acting through dance and twins were in such high demand in the entertainment industry, my mother signed us up with an extras casting agency to pursue acting opportunities in Los Angeles.

While working in the entertainment industry, I noticed that resources were slim for a majority of those who did not work under the Screen Actors Guild - American Federation of Television and Radio Artists (SAG-AFTRA). Television and film extras were separated into two camps: "union" and "non-union". On one hand, those who were in the union (SAG-AFTRA) were protected under the law with formal contracts where they could negotiate wages and gain easier access to job opportunities. On the other hand, "non-union" extras did not have access to the same protections. The lack of a formal contract subjected workers to the bare minimum in terms of employment, such as the minimum wage law of the state and a lack of available resources to assist in obtaining jobs. In addition, the expensive membership fees and onerous admission requirements made entry into the union very difficult for non-union entertainers looking for better pay and benefit opportunities. One such requirement was that non-union entertainers needed to obtain three "union paychecks" in order to be eligible for admission into the union. These instances of obtaining a union paycheck were very rare occasions for non-union extras. At times, they were obtained when either a director randomly chose to extend all cast members a union paystub or a non-union worker possessed a rare trait (such as being a twin) that was sought out by the producers.

Obtaining a union job was like winning a golden ticket in the sense that these jobs were very scarce. Unfortunately, a majority of my peers fell into the non-union category and due to the low pay and working conditions, had no choice but to obtain employment elsewhere or quit the industry altogether. In a sense, my Hollywood peers seemingly had no voice. As a non-union extra working part time with very similar struggles, I was instantly inspired to seek a way in which I could advocate for these incredibly talented and ambitious entertainers via the law. Over the years after college, I sought out legal employment opportunities involving entertainment where I eventually learned that I could make a difference via the law.

My appreciation for the arts, along with witnessing the injustices of the industry have helped me find my own voice and inspired me to pursue a career where I can amplify the voice of others in an industry where they often are not heard when they try to speak for themselves. As a future attorney, my career goal is to assist entertainers who lack a voice - or access to resources, particularly legal resources - to get adequate protections in Hollywood. While I could not aid my colleagues while working beside them as an extra, I am excited about the work that I am going to be able to do for them as an entertainment attorney.

Appendix F: Diversity Statement Samples

<u>Sample One: Growing Up Biracial</u>

I am a mixed black woman. The product of a once forbidden love, a dirty secret. I am diversity, I am integration. I do not fit into one box, nor could I simply check one on an application. To do so would ask me to be a fraction of myself. My truth is complex. My identity even more so. It is time for this country to make space for me.

I am a mixed black woman. An identity that has taken me 21 years to solidify, to embrace, to confidently share, to know, to understand, to *be*. From the tender age of six I remember walking through restaurants alongside my baby brother to be seated at a dinner table with my white mom's hand in one and my black dad's hand in the other, confused as to why everyone stared at our little family of four. Quizzical faces of confusion looked on as we made our way to our table for an all too familiar uncomfortable public outing. It wasn't until I grew older that I became aware of why it was that we couldn't seem to go anywhere in public without silent stares, whispers, and the like. Because together, our family was confusing;   we didn't make sense. Two light-skinned babies, who quite frankly looked Hispanic or Latino, with a blonde-haired, blue-eyed, fair-skinned white woman, and a tall slender black man right beside her. Countless memories live rent-free in my mind of my dad being stopped in public, interrogated on who I belonged to, questioned if he was my grandfather or if I was adopted. The all too familiar pain of jolting forward as the car slammed to a 20-mph speed at the sight of a police officer passing by as my dad drove me to school in the mornings. Women approached my mother, speaking in Spanish to us as if we didn't belong to the white woman carrying us through the toy isle. Her constant response? "Yes, she is my daughter".

I did not fully embrace my identity as a mixed black woman until college, but it took a lot of personal trial and error to get there. All my life I had been too white for the black people and too black for the white people. Ostracized by both of the communities that make up my identity. My curly hair was "too soft" for me to be black, I didn't "sound black", I "acted white"; all of these are just a fraction of the micro aggressions I faced as a child. This left me somewhere in the middle, and in small town rural Virginia, there was no middle. There were never

158

other children who looked like me or who had parents that looked like mine. This led to a lot of unanswered questions, a constant identity crisis; a battle between two selves. As a young girl it was lonely, confusing, and isolating to have no sense of community, to not feel seen.

This confusion and frustration only turned into anger and guilt as I navigated my identity through college. Arriving at a predominantly white institution such as Penn State, I was surrounded by strangers who obviously didn't know who my parents were or what my family looked like. But even then, I thought coming to a large university I would surely see so many people that looked like me and who shared similar experiences to my own. I was grossly mistaken. A few weeks in, after seeing virtually nobody I could physically relate to, I figured it would be easy to blend in with the majority, to pass as white so that I wouldn't feel ostracized or othered. But it wasn't that simple, a white identity was projected onto me not only by my white peers but also by members of the black community at Penn State as well. I was all too used to this from my childhood experiences but something inside of me desired to be known, to be seen, and to be heard.

Being on a fairly "liberal" campus as a mixed black woman trying to solidify my identity within myself and outwardly to others made this experience difficult to say the very least. Especially as I began to navigate my passion for social justice, race relations, criminal justice reform, and police reform. To the black community I was a poser, a privileged light-skin trying to fit in where I didn't belong, trying to relate to oppression I could never understand in their eyes. To the white community I was confused, and I was confusing them, making most of them uncomfortable with my ideas, my beliefs, my values, the simple fact that I considered myself black. I felt oppressed like the marginalized group that makes up half of my identity but never felt embraced or affirmed by that same group. This experience has been paralyzing and silencing. But I will not be silenced any longer. I refuse to compare struggles, to pretend that I too haven't suffered from racism, oppression, and discrimination. The truth about my experience as a mixed black woman is that both the privileged and the oppressed live

159

inside of me. That while I experience privilege, I also experience pain. I reckon with duality and contradiction unconsciously on a daily basis. This has only been heightened in our nation's current social climate. It is almost impossible to explain the experience of watching your country try to acknowledge what has been my normal and my reality all of my life. Figuring out how to hold both pain and progress in one place, how to heal a racial divide entwined in my DNA from conception. This experience has been both liberating and exhausting, triggering and healing, beautiful and painful.

As a mixed black woman with a Juris Doctorate, I plan to use my privilege to pave the way for those who don't have my privilege, who don't have a voice, or those who haven't been allowed a voice or a seat at the table. I plan to pass the microphone when it is not mine to hold, when someone's cries are louder than my own. I want to consistently be aware of my privilege so that it does not get in the way of my purpose; my desire to be a beacon of light for marginalized communities. I belong on the front lines of social justice activism, public policy, and criminal justice reform. I am already my ancestors' wildest dream, but law school will make those dreams a reality for myself, my parents, *all* of the communities I belong to, black, white, and mixed, for future generations to come.

Sample Two: Growing Up Low-Income and With Parents that Immigrated to the Country

I remember growing up in a predominately low income and Spanish speaking area of Arlington, VA with my immigrant family. As a child, I never found it odd that my parents were immigrants, spoke English with heavy accents, and were minimally educated. My mother arrived in the United States from Cuba and Barbados at a young age. Although she was unfamiliar with the language, she partook in American customs while in densely diverse New York City. My father arrived to the U.S. from Nicaragua, along with his siblings and parents. He came under political asylum, as my grandfather was part of military forces that attempted to keep the Sandinistas from overthrowing the existing government. My father worked hard to take advantage of the

160

opportunities that the United States offered such as being able to establish his business. While my parents were working, I was afforded the opportunity to be under the care of both my Cuban/Bajan and Nicaraguan grandparents.

I spent my summers in New York City with my Cuban/Bajan grandparents but primarily lived with my Nicaraguan grandparents. I was able to form an identity that reflected two Latin American and West Indian cultures through ethnicity and social influences. My Nicaraguan grandparents lived in a suburb of Washington, D.C., called South Arlington. South Arlington, although surrounded by the affluence of the Nation's Capital, was dangerous, drug and crime ridden. My grandparents settled there as it was the most affordable in the area when they first arrived to this country. But nevertheless, it was what I considered home. I grew up there surrounded by my culture which afforded me the opportunity to appreciate it once I became an adult.

There was no difference between ICE and the police in my neighborhood. I would often see families be displaced due to immigration concerns. Many of these families' main source of income / sole provider would be deported, often leaving the children to run the household, which at times led to choosing a life of crime. As an adolescent, I would support my friends whose parent was getting deported. I felt a moral obligation to be there for them in their time of need. All I could do was provide my friends with kindness and comfortability. At that time, I was too young to know it, but my actions, which were led by compassion and integrity, were core values that later became inherent to my persona.

I ended up joining the U.S. Army, as a first generation servicemember in my family. My diversity unfolded in various ways. It took some time to integrate my experiences as a first-generation Afro-Latino who had only learned English a few years before joining. I did not find too many peers who were like me. I did not fit the mold of a stereotypical Latino because of my looks, but I also did not feel fully connected to the West Indian or African American soldiers as I was raised primarily in a   Latin American environment. I longed for belonging. I avoided speaking about my culture to others out of being ashamed of who I was. I longed for belonging into the American culture like everyone surrounding me. Out of shame, I attempted to assume a 100% American identity without the Latin American culture   and attempted to blend in with others.

Once I had children, I began to realize that I could no longer erase my culture or upbringing. Rather, I wanted to make sure they understood their ancestral history. I had to grasp the ideology that my racial and socioeconomic background was not any different than others. I was just blessed to have been raised in a multicultural environment that allowed me to stand out through experiences. These experiences became the prerequisite of pride and strength that I displayed to my children to understand their background.

As I got older, I began to value my identity and the significance of my diversity. I learned to develop and use my voice to speak up for issues that my community was enduring such as racial profiling, immigration issues and other social injustices. Over time, I came to the realization that I needed to embrace my diversity rather than suppress it. As I embark on a legal education, my experiences, not just as a person of color, but as a bicultural daughter of West Indian and Latino immigrants, can help contribute to the law school's environment as well as the legal field. My voice can display a different perspective of representation, as well as a diversity of thought in a field where people of color are underrepresented.

Sample Three: Helping Dad Navigate the Legal System

I followed closely behind my father when he was called to the podium. Before the age of 15, as the eldest daughter of an immigrant family, I had helped negotiate car prices, interpreted during life-altering medical appointments, and sorted financial issues within my family and the Mexican community. I could easily navigate city ordinances and locate resources to help solve almost any problem. The English and Spanish languages were my tools and I wielded their power to overcome barriers for accessing these resources. Hundreds of times over, I understood the importance of bridging the gaps in a conversation between ESL Mexican family and community members and

162

monolingual English-speakers at the grocery store, car dealerships, and hospital and court appointments. Yet in this moment, as we stood before the arraigning judge without a lawyer, I was without tools. I did not speak the language of the law in the courtroom. The Michigan flag bore Latin; the bailiff stood guard; the glossy antique cherry finish of the wooden panels exalted the judge's incomprehensible words.

"And, who are you?" the judge grumbled. Standing next to my dad, I bent the microphone toward me. "I'm here to interpret for my father," I said nervously looking past the judge's confused glare at the courtroom's prestigious seal behind him. The physical and linguistic variants of this legal language were pronounced as the judge and my father looked to me for help. Soon after, we were ushered into a room to meet with a prosecutor who urged him to accept a plea bargain. I turned to my dad and we decided to consult with a lawyer.

As we left the courtroom, I resolved that I would be better equipped to aid members of my community going forward by familiarizing myself with relevant legal terminology. I could not practice law, but I could dive into the minds of renowned ancient Roman and Greek legal philosophers. I thus decided to continue pursuing Latin for two more years in high school in addition to signing up for Ancient Greek. Wanting to learn more about one of the most influential legal systems of ancient society, I dug beyond our coursework to discover the defense speech of Marcus Tullius Cicero. Cicero's role in Pro Roscio Amerino as a defense attorney for a man accused of patricide inspired me to dual enroll in criminal justice courses at Madonna University, where I became engrossed in legal interpretation and in seeing the nuances of interpretation within each opinion, concurrence, and dissent.

The power of language interpretation that I observed at an early age has stayed with me throughout my academic endeavors and community advocacy. As a classically trained sociologist and future lawyer, I apply to law school knowing that the ability to successfully and simultaneously interpret a multiplicity of languages—whether culturally or contextually—bears significant moral and developmental ramifications upon resolutions sought for all parties being served;

163

whether this involves local municipalities aiming to achieve concise language for legislation addressing the challenges of immigrant communities, or merely a young 15-year-old girl interpreting for her father in legal proceedings. I want to help shape legal policies that will help individuals, communities, and organizations work collaboratively and effectively at bridging cultural gaps. I want to live a life promoting a monumental shift across institutions toward symmetric, and, ultimately, human rights.

Sample Four: Passion for Dismantling the School-To-Prison Pipeline

Justice is a word that I wish could be concretely defined and associated with equity. Instead, it is a term that I consider pretty elusive, especially, in this day and age of widely expressed racism, bigotry, and divisiveness in a democratic system that is supposed to render impartiality. It is no secret that Black & Brown communities face a number of disparities & inequitable disadvantages from basic healthcare to housing and beyond. Inequalities in the education system didn't end when segregation did. And society is now criminalizing our young Black and Brown boys and girls as is seen via the School to Prison Pipeline. As I pursue my law degree, my goal is to someday dismantle the "disciplinary" policies that lead to this phenomenon.

Until serving the community of Newark, NJ (which is high crime & poverty stricken) as an educator, I was not aware of the true detriment of the School to Prison Pipeline. Sadly, it is a reality in Newark and in many other urban cities. Reinforcement of the School to Prison Pipeline comes in many fashions dressed up as seemingly face-neutral school policies: dress codes, excessive & harsh disciplinary actions, zero tolerance policies, the overuse of standardized tests, heighted use of policing via school resources officers (SROs), surveillance, and so much more. For example, I had an eighth-grade student on house arrest. I also had a student who wasn't allowed in class and had to sit in the office the entire school day because her shoelaces weren't black. I had to administer standardized exams every six weeks. And I escorted middle schoolers, ages 11-14, to class every class in a silent single file line in a building that one could easily navigate on their own in all of seven minutes or less. As the school year progressed my work setting seemed less like a safe, supportive, and fun learning environment, but more like a juvenile detention or behavioral center.

In the pursuit of my law degree, my desire is to dismantle the injustices in our school systems by maximizing the role of activism, specifically with regard to K-12 advocacy. In light of the social justice movement happening right now we are fighting for our humanity, I believe this fight must include the humanity of our young scholars. Much of society has seen the videos of cops slamming Black & Brown students to the ground in the classroom, against lockers, and or handcuffing them for minor and non-criminal matters or offenses. And this hasn't happened just to older children. Elementary students are also experiencing the same horrors. The criminalization of our students must stop. That is why I want to enact and activate change. Change to standardized testing strategies. Change to the method of scoring tests that is used to fund schools and build prisons. Change the Zero Tolerance policies. Change to the isolation and seclusion of students as a disciplinary action. Change to the behavior of policing in schools. And change to the way Black and Brown students are viewed as criminals, threating, and future inmates instead of future change makers.

Sample Five: Navigating Microaggressions in the Workplace

I was the only black woman in the law firm - often mislabeled as mean, aggressive, and anti-social by my peers. I was wrongly accused of stealing and misusing the team credit card, (although I never had access to it) and ridiculed for dressing in formal attire in a casual setting. I found myself explaining and defending myself repeatedly.

The anti-black and racially motivated criticism persisted and continued to worsen over time, turning into isolation. For example, the paralegals were often broken into teams to work on specific projects. In one instance, there was a project that I was assigned to collaborate on with two of my peers. I was excited to work on this project; however, it ended up being a missed opportunity. The team held meetings and discussed details of the cases without me, not allowing me to contribute. Although I was always well prepared for our broader case discussions, I felt stripped of the opportunity to present my findings in smaller group settings.

Eventually, I decided to address the microaggressions, seeming misogyny, and stereotyping with my colleague one-on-one to discuss how we could cultivate a better working relationship. Although I expected it to be a productive conversation, it quickly turned negative, and I was unexpectedly accused of being confrontational. Afterward, I was targeted even further. Attempts to share my side of the story were not welcomed and fell on deaf ears. I felt powerless.

In Jamaica, we say, "If you cyaa get turkey, satisfy wid John Crow," which means: make the best of any situation and be content with what you have. Growing up, I was not accustomed to harping on adversities. So despite the challenges I faced, I continued to persevere, continuously looking ahead at my goals, and quietly trying to disprove the labels that had been placed on me. In hindsight, I recognize how my upbringing contributed to my silence. My need to keep my job to take care of my family prevented me from speaking up sooner.

Despite my negative experiences, I excelled in my role and was mentored by one of the firm's top attorneys. Although I was moving up in my career, I did not feel empowered to speak up for fear of retaliation or termination. Before long, the constant belittling began to wear on my spirit, and I resigned from the firm.

Upon reflection, I would not have done anything differently. My experience in the firm has allowed me to explore how to push beyond my limits and thrive in the face of blatant discrimination. I now know that my need to speak up and contribute is not anger or aggression. It is the passion necessary to help me fight and advocate for others.

Sample Six: Being a Queer, Black Woman Teacher

When I first started teaching, as a Black queer woman in a predominantly Black and Brown low-income school in Texas, I was so afraid of what it'd look like to be authentically me. I was nervous

166

about coming out to my coworkers, sharing my life and politics with my kids, and just existing. I remember in my first week, at an human resources training, one of the facilitators shared the story of a teacher in another Texas district who was fired when her school found out she worked out at a pole fitness studio. The message was clear, to be a teacher meant no parts of your personal life were off limits, so I decided to hide.

Soon after that training, I attended an content training where we learned a concept called windows and mirrors. This concept asserts that in order for students to be engaged in their learning they need a good balance of the two. Windows refer to content that encourages and allows students to look into and learn about identities and worlds beyond what is familiar to them. Whereas mirrors refer to content that reflects back to students their own identities and the places they come from. In theory, windows help students build empathy and community, and mirrors help them understand themselves and their unique place in their community. The concept mostly applies to building classroom libraries and deciding on content materials, but in that first year, it became how I understood myself in relation to my students and my coworkers.

As expected in any middle school classroom, my students started off the year super inquisitive about my life. A few of them even flat out asked me if I was gay. I evaded the question, saying it was inappropriate and irrelevant to both my ability to teach and theirs to learn. Eventually, they dropped it, and so did I. Toward the middle of the school year, there was an incident where a Black queer student was maliciously outed to her parent, a coach at the school, by another teacher. My heart broke imagining how isolated and unsafe she must have felt in that moment.

For a week, I couldn't rest so I scheduled a meeting with the principal to discuss my outrage at the situation and at our school for having a culture where something like that could happen in the first place. I was told to mind my business and that the role of a teacher was simply to deliver content, but I knew it was too late for that. By week two of the school year, I had built relationships with all of my students that were strong enough to tear down a wall. I knew my student needed someone to fight for her. She needed a mirror, and my coworkers needed a window. The next day, I came out to my coworkers and my students. By the end of that week, at least ten of my students had come out to me as queer, curious, or gender fluid, and I realized the power in my identity. Not only did my queer students deserve to see me fully and know that it's ok to be Black and queer, but it was important that the rest of the school, students, and staff to know that as well.

Now, at the beginning of each school year, the very first assignment I give my students is an "about me" collage project. I give them a rubric with all the things I want them to include, and I do my first lesson of the year on pronouns. From my first year, I learned how important it is to establish my classroom as a safe space not only for my students and the multitude of identities that they hold, but also for myself. Voices and identities like mine and my students' deserve to exist and should exist freely both in the classroom and the workspace. Unfortunately, I've seen first-hand the harm that can happen when they don't. Being a Black queer woman has afforded me such a unique perspective on life, community, advocacy, and justice. I am excited to stand tall in all of my identities as I begin law school.

Sample Seven: Being a [Former] Black Republican

"Give this young man a hand," Tucker Carlson shouted into his microphone. He wanted to congratulate me on winning a state title in Oratorical Speaking. I was the only black person in attendance, so it wasn't hard for the hundreds of eyes to locate me. I was ushered to my feet so that the entire crowd of middle-aged white conservatives could ogle me up close. As I bashfully waved back to the roaring crowd, Mr. Hannity proudly proclaimed that people like me would carry the torch of conservatism forward. Little did he know, I had already removed the small red elephant pin from my suit. I was no conservative.

As a black kid from the north side of El Paso, Texas, a city notorious for perpetuating racism and "traditional" Southern values, I regularly heard people imply that black people were lazy and incapable

168

of adding anything of significant value to society. I often felt inadequate and embarrassed standing in free food lines with my family at all-white churches. My feelings of inadequacy led me to seek out opportunities to gain their acceptance, in hopes that I would be shielded from the derision evoked by my black skin.

My opportunity came after being selected by my high school debate coach to represent East Texas in the "Texas Sons of the American Revolution State Oration Contest." I worked tirelessly on a five-minute speech centered around a slave named James Armistead and how he, despite being enslaved, somehow embodied traditional American values. I won first place. At the ceremonial dinner, dozens of complete strangers came up to me to shake my hand. With every hand I shook, I felt as if I was earning my right to associate with those on the south side of my hometown. Among those people was the Smith County Republican Party chairman, who eagerly invited me to speak at the group's next meeting in El Paso concerning values that I felt were important to black conservatives. I had never thought of myself as conservative but I obliged in hopes of gaining more acceptance. I traveled back home with a red elephant pin and a new identity that ultimately wasn't mine.

The speech at the party meeting went well; I remembered and regurgitated the list of conservative values I had found online. Consequently, several attendees invited me to speak at various events they had planned. But each speaking invitation came with a caveat – I was to only speak on topics they deemed important. With every speech I presented, I told myself I was proving my worth as a black man, but I was doing the opposite. I was prevented from addressing my concerns on the pernicious racial disparities in El Paso. I was discouraged from sharing experiences of racism and mistreatment as it didn't fit the "narrative" they wanted to construct. They argued that systematic racism was a myth, while I had seen firsthand the impact it had had on black people, including myself.

It was at the event with Tucker Carlson that I decided to be who I really was. I chose to embrace truth instead of the short-term thrill of acceptance. I learned to take pride in my real-life story and in my unique set of priorities and values as a black man. I had enough; I was done promoting views that were in stark contrast to my own. I permanently removed the small red elephant pin from my suit.

This experience taught me to take pride in my life story and unique set of priorities and values as a black man. From that moment forward, I have used my voice to preach my own truth. At law school, I will devote myself to encouraging my peers to uphold their own inherent value systems. I will uplift others in taking courageous action to defy negative societal pressures, even if it means sacrificing a potential opportunity. More importantly, I will help inspire a generation to walk to the beat of their own drums by using my story as an example. Our true identity is the source of our intrinsic value as human beings. I don't need to wear a pin to be somebody – instead, I will proudly wear my black skin.

Sample Eight: Growing up Low-Income & Balancing Work and School

My family immigrated in the early years of my life, prompted by the unstable political circumstances of our home country. Venezuela's dictator had recently come to power, dismantling democratic institutions, and taking political prisoners. My mother publicly opposed the new regime and used her knowledge as an attorney to push back on many of these changes. When the situation grew worse, my parents moved our family to Miami, Florida.

As young immigrant parents starved for cash, my parents began working immediately after we arrived in the United States. Although my mother practiced law in Venezuela, she was unable to return to school to pursue law in the states. Nevertheless, she raised me to embody diligence, intelligence, and endurance. She shared that these qualities were significant to her career back home.

Growing up in Miami, I was surrounded by a lively Latin American community. Most of our friends also belonged to families that had fled their dangerous homelands. Despite painful histories, the Latin culture was apparent through shared food, music, and a sense of camaraderie. As a kid, I felt connected to my heritage as a first-

170

generation immigrant. Despite never returning to where I came from, I felt that I belonged among the Hispanic customs, language, and people that engulfed my Florida hometown.

In my teen years, our family moved to Texas, where I began working part-time in high school to save money for college. My first job was as a waitress at a restaurant, where I worked 10 hours a week serving barbecue and cleaning tables. Since that first job, I have continued working in different roles while studying during community college and university. I now work to pay for my own living and education expenses as a self-sufficient student. At one point in my junior year, I balanced a couple of part-time jobs, student ambassador work, a legislative internship at the state capitol, and my classes. I managed well because I have been subconsciously training myself for this workload. The past six years of working and studying have helped me build endurance to achieve my desired outcomes. Engagement in multiple academic and professional pursuits has become second nature to me.

I strive to be a professional Latina woman, just like my mother was. Throughout my life, I have come to value her traits of diligence, intelligence, and endurance in my endeavors.

Sample Nine: Growing up in a Drug & Crime Infested Community

The life experiences of someone from south Arizona, specifically the border is truly unique. As portrayed in movies and shows of Mexican Americans being caught in between two dominant cultures – Mexican and American – there is truth to these tropes. Growing up I never realized that my childhood was different from others'. My hometown of Yuma, Arizona is more than 96% Hispanic and a majority of us are impacted by the same things. The city is located in one of the poorest counties in the state, and is a place where education isn't highly valued. As a kid I used to work construction during summers with my dad in order help provide for my household and save money. It was tough work, but I knew that my work would mean more money for my family, so I did it proudly.

171

With time, I learned a great deal not just about construction but about the types of lives my co-workers lived. Many were undocumented, and as we sat on empty dirt lots eating our lunch, they would talk to me about their families and the sorts of challenges they faced. These summers are where I became cognizant of immigration, and how merely being born on this side of the border meant a drastically different life and set of opportunities. My dad used to tell me stories of how my grandpa used to go from state to state as a migrant farm worker and construction worker. One of the reasons why my dad would take me to work was to see how hard of a life it was. I used to see my dad work ten hours a day in 100+ degree weather, but he never complained.

I think the culmination of my experiences can bring to light the struggles and realities of a border town Mexican American. Because the Mexican American experience is not a monolith and can be very different when you grow up in a border town as compared to a suburb or big city, I think that by being included in your incoming class I can be a partial voice for the millions like me. This group often doesn't fit into the standard Mexican American category, and too often our voices are never heard. This group deals with the influence of cartels on our communities, immigration woes, a lack of education, and a culture that is not entirely American nor Mexican. Topics like these are important in discussing this area of the country and its people. The communities on the border are growing at a rapid pace, with many residents branching out into many major metropolitan areas throughout the country. Thus, helping others to understand these communities is an immediate way that I can enhance the intellectual life of your law school community.

The topics of immigration and border security have never been more widely discussed than they are now. It is imperative that discussions centered on finding solutions to the problems facing this population include those who are closest to said problems and those who deal with these issues every day. Unfortunately, too often, lawmakers and politicians from non-border states talk of "solutions" to things they lack an intimate understanding of. My experience at the AUSA office in Arizona and my upbringing has allowed me to have a

172

unique perspective that I believe would benefit both the legal profession and policy discussions. I've worked countless criminal and civil cases and feel like my grasp of the legal side of this area is particularly strong. I believe that this experience combined with my personal familiarity with border-town experiences will go a long way in dealing with the problems that affect communities like mine.

As discussed briefly in my personal statement, I have experienced some truly heartbreaking things throughout my life. That is one of the reasons I desire to become an attorney and why I am so passionate about pursuing this path. Sadly, I have had family, friends, and co-workers here one day and deported the next. I've seen the effects of human trafficking through the exploitation of migrant workers in my community and have unfortunately seen the effects of sex trafficking on the biological mother of my niece. I feel like sharing these experiences with my peers and classmates will go a long way in aiding students and fellow future lawyers like me who want to better understand or work in the realm of immigration-related public interest work.

Sample Ten: Growing up Poor, Queer, in the Hood, and with an Incarcerated Parent

I grew up on the west side of Chicago, predominately know as one of the city's most dangerous and notorious neighborhoods. My life was not "perfect" because my mom raised me alone because of my father's incarceration. I frequently saw drug dealers on corners, shooting dice for fun, and thought at one point that this was going to be my life. I often heard loud police sirens because someone in my neighborhood was either arrested or gunned down. For a long time, I feared that I would either end up in jail or dead one day.

Growing up, I watched as my mom used all her resources to put me through grammar and high school as she went off to work to make a stable living for us. At one point, when I was a pre-teen, I believed that we were on an upper trajectory to success until one day, that dream was crushed. The apartment we lived in was vandalized and raided by robbers, and everything that my mom worked hard for was either stolen or trashed. I watched as she tearfully gathered a few of our belongings that were left and decided that we would go to live with my grandmother, who also stayed on the west side. I struggled with the new reality of not having my room for years, not even a bed to sleep in at night. I knew this wasn't the life that I wanted for us, so when I was 10, I told my mom that I would make sure we never had to live like this ever again. I promised her that I would make a difference for both of us.

While growing up poor and with an incarcerated father came with its own set of challenges, so too did being a queer Black man living in "the hood." I was around five years old when I first discovered my sexuality. I knew I wanted to make a difference in the world. However, I had to deal with many complications when it came to educating my family and my community on what it means to be black and queer and how those two identities can co-exist at the same time. I always had to deal with complex questions like "do you think you were born this way" or "how can you be black and queer and still push the black agenda." I consistently had to fight to tell my peers that I could do both and fight for human rights because I am a human first. The reality is that being queer has not been an easy ride; in a world of academia and many different perspectives, I have consistently challenged myself to become a better-educated person in this community. These experiences will allow me to bring a diverse perspective to the classroom and allow for appropriate discourse regarding race, sexuality, and gender.

Appendix G: Resume Sample

NAME
City, State | Cell: xxx-xxx-xxxx| email

EDUCATION:

Bernard M. Baruch College, Weissman School of Arts and Sciences   New York, NY
Bachelor of Arts in Political Science, Minor Black Studies   Received May 2017
Academic Honors: *Summa Cum Laude* and Dean's List every semester

---

WORK EXPERIENCE:

Deloitte, Washington, DC — *Senior Policy Analyst* | **July 2021 - Present**
- Closely monitor and flag legislative and regulatory actions that could impact the firm
- Advocate the firm's policy positions at conferences, in meetings, and internally
- Craft and execute the firm's legislative and political strategy at the state and federal levels
- Conduct research, provide analysis, and prepare presentations explaining the political, societal, and legislative dynamics of a wide range of policy issues including health, climate change and technology
- Work directly with leadership providing project management support, assisting with intake, tracking, and execution of requests and projects

Deloitte, Arlington, VA — *Regulatory & Legislative Analyst* | **June 2019 - July 2021**
- Drafted constituent response letters on immigration, healthcare, and consumer protection
- Researched federal legislation and regulations to analyze the impact on the firm's business objectives
- Created risk sensing alerts utilizing data trends and volume to develop policy insights for leadership
- Served as a liaison to internal teams and key regulators to identify cross-collaboration opportunities
- Coordinated weekly and ad hoc reports covering major policy issues that the firm monitored for internal use such as data privacy, artificial intelligence, corporate activism, and racial equity

Office of Senator Sherrod Brown (D-OH), Washington, DC — *Staff Assistant* | **April 2018 - June 2019**
- Drafted constituent response letters on immigration, healthcare, and consumer protection
- Supervised interns and conducted various training for optimum performance
- Gathered feedback from constituents on pending legislation brought before the Senate
- Monitored bills and prepared memorandum for appropriate legislative staffers

Office of Rep. Adriano Espaillat (D-NY), Washington, DC — *Legislative Intern* | **Jan 2018 - April 2018**
- Administered immigration and education policy research to assist staffers with legislative proposals
- Drafted event speech material for community gatherings with a focus on regional leadership
- Scheduled meetings with constituents and prepared detailed itineraries for the Congressman

Congressional Black Caucus Foundation, Washington, DC — *Emerging Leader* | **Jan 2018 - April 2018**
- Served within a cohort of 24 Congressional Black Caucus Foundation fellows
- Worked with senior staff on career development activities specific to service on Capitol Hill
- Attended legislative briefings tailored to service in the House of Representatives

Marwood Group, New York, NY — *Legal Assistant* | **Jan 2017 - Dec 2017**
- Performed LLC state license renewals to advise various private equity firms
- Completed research on healthcare statutes and regulatory compliance for client awareness
- Facilitated a comprehensive dialogue to ensure that financial metrics were met and reviewed

Baldonado & Associates, P.C. New York, NY — *Legal Intern* | **Aug 2016 - Dec 2016**
- Supported the contracts and negotiation process under the guidance of senior legal counsel
- Prepared and executed social media marketing campaigns for clients
- Performed administrative tasks such as responding to calls and organizing meetings with clients

New York Supreme Court, Kings County Integrated Domestic Violence Court, Brooklyn, NY — *Judicial Intern* | **Jan 2016 - June 2016**
- Conducted background research to prepare case briefs for principal court attorneys
- Analyzed case transcripts to support judge in current court proceedings
- Observed civil and criminal cases to identify methods used by attorneys to defend their clients

VOLUNTEER EXPERIENCE:

Embassy of Haiti, Washington, D.C. — *Event Volunteer* | **Jan 2018 – Present**
- Encouraged people to be active in the Haitian community through organizational events and projects
- Ensured that event space was kept clean and organized at all times
- Provided physical and logistical support to presenters and over 200 event attendees

Mayor Bill de Blasio Campaign, Brooklyn, NY — *Canvasser* | **Aug 2017 - Nov 2017**
- Participated in door to door communication with potential voters in a friendly manner
- Educated potential voters on candidate's political platform and answered any questions they had
- Documented voter information for data analysis and campaign planning

Haitian American Caucus, Brooklyn, NY — *Fundraising/Event Volunteer* | **Jan 2016 - Dec 2017**
- Developed fundraising marketing strategies in coordination with volunteer team members
- Furnished logistical support for fundraising presentations and events
- Organized workshop to educate undocumented Haitians of their legal rights

LEADERSHIP EXPERIENCE:

Baruch Pre-Law Society, New York, NY — *Executive Board Secretary* | **August 2016 - May 2017**
- Supported board administrative tasks by managing calendar and coordinating events
- Responded to and routed emails to appropriate authorized personnel in a timely matter
- Updated and maintained the database for all office records and documents
- Developed and maintained strong relationships with other clubs for future co-sponsorship

EXTRACURRICULAR ACTIVITIES:
Baruch Pre-Law Society, *Member* — August 2015 - May 2016
Baruch Sigma Alpha Delta Honor Society, *Member* — August 2016 - May 2017
Baruch Black Student Union, *Member* — August 2015 - May 2017
Baruch Caribbean Student Association, *Member* — August 2015 - May 2017

ORGANIZATIONS:
Legally BLK Fund, *Scholar/Member* — August 2020 - Present
Senate Black Legislative Staff Caucus, *Member* — April 2018 - June 2019

SKILLS/INTERESTS:
Languages: Intermediate in Haitian Creole
Personal Interests: Cooking, Painting, Biking, Yoga, Travel, Music, Health/Wellness Blogging

Appendix H: Why XYZ School Essay Samples

<u>Sample One: Why NYU Essay</u>

I first came to know of NYU Law after looking into the background of Congressman Hakeem Jeffries. I've followed Congressman Jeffries career since 2017 and admired how he conducted himself along with the stances he had towards different political topics. After learning that he had attended NYU Law, I researched the school more and was amazed about everything NYU offered. I felt that NYU was everything I wanted in a school and that the school's programming would best set me up for success.

One of the reasons for why NYU pertains to the Southern District of New York externship. I have worked multiple years with the USAO in my hometown, I have learned a great deal about the incredible work done at the SDNY and the caliber of attorneys within. I hope to one day become an AUSA and being able to gain practical experience while learning from some of the most accomplished AUSA's in the country is something that I dearly value. In addition, having the opportunity to take courses with former AUSA for the SDNY and Adjunct Professor Preet Bharara is something that no other school can offer. I can't think of a better combination of faculty and externship opportunities like that at NYU.

NYU's combination of public interest clinics along with its incredible LRAP Plus is something that has also caught my attention. A strong reason why I hope to become an attorney is to work within the immigration and human rights fields. NYU's incredible clinical offerings such as its Immigrant Rights Clinic, Immigration Defense Clinic, and The Future of Human Rights Practicum would allow me to be involved in work that matters a great deal to me. In Addition, having the opportunity to learn under a human rights expert like Cesar Rodriguez-Garavito would be truly rewarding to me. The opportunities that come with having access to LRAP Plus can't be understated. The type of work that motivates me towards becoming an attorney doesn't lend itself to big paydays. LRAP Plus would allow me to pursue my goals without having to worry about the finances as much.

I love everything that being an NYU law student can offer, and feel that being an NYU alum will mean as much as it does the second I graduate and 40 years from now. Being in a melting pot like New York, and close to NGOs like Human Rights First, ACLU, Inter-American Commission on Human Rights amongst the many others is truly exciting. Lastly, I believe that NYU is the school that can best prepare me for the path that I am on. Your reputation for being the premier public interest school in the country at the center of the public interest mecca that is New York is well-founded. I look forward to potentially learning under world-renowned legal scholars that call NYU home and look forward to collaborating with the incredible students that NYU is known to attract.

Sample Two: Why Michigan Essay

Michigan Law's appeal was solidified after a phone conversation with Assistant Director of Admissions Erik Choisy regarding the unique focus on inclusion that Michigan Law strives towards. It was through Erik's explanation of valuing diversity with the intent to produce meaningful change that I discovered Michigan's commitment in preparing students to develop inclusive and comprehensive perspectives that are suited for serving all people. Where Michigan Law distinguishes itself to me is through its dedication to preparing a diverse student body to protect varying types of vulnerable individuals through public service, an area that I know well.

Michigan Law presents me with the opportunity to protect the vulnerable through several varying channels. I look forward to taking up this charge by assuming the role of a lawyer in the Community Enterprise Clinic where I will assist local business owners in registering trademarks and services, as well as encourage local governments to fix disparities in internet and cellular availability that plagued many of my low-income customers at Verizon. I anticipate working alongside my peers in the Pro Bono Program and taking on real-world assignments to represent at-risk youth in fighting for a second chance through Michigan's Juvenile Justice Clinic. In addition, I am eager to serve as a mentor to underrepresented high school students in the Ann Abor and Detroit area.

Furthermore, I am intent to engage in the transformative extracurricular activities offered by Michigan. I plan on continuing my debate career through Michigan's Moot Court team, advocating for cryptocurrency and blockchain developments through Michigan's Technology Law Review, and working with the Office of Student Life to develop a student led organization that builds the bridge between blockchain enthusiasts, blockchain development, and technology law. In addition, I look forward to one day working with Michigan Law's Black Law Student Association and Michigan Law's administration to develop outreach initiatives to assist in finding diverse talent to fill future incoming classes.

I look forward to what Michigan Law and the Ann Arbor area have to offer me (I am especially excited for the front row seats to the Michigan vs Ohio State rivalry football games). But I am even more excited to offer everything I can to Michigan Law.

Sample Three: Why Berkeley Essay

I was born and raised in the San Francisco Bay Area. This community nourished my love and passion for the environment. When I was younger my parents also made a point to take our entire family on nature outings like sailing in the Bay and camping in Mendocino. On most of our trips, I rarely saw other Black families out in nature. After a particularly inspiring trip to the Amazon rainforest in Ecuador I realized that my passion in life was to protect and serve as an advocate for the environment.

Berkeley Law has one of the leading Environmental Law programs in the nation, with The Center for Law, Energy & the Environment. CLEE is particularly attractive to me because I recognize the urgency to establish strong legal support systems to protect our environment with a specific and intense focus on climate change. I have long been an advocate of implementing environmentally sustainable models for development.

Currently, I am interested in sustainable development and renewable energy, specifically looking at how we can get creative with international policies that promote and support long-term solutions to climate change. Because of this interest, I am particularly excited about the opportunity to take classes such as International Environmental Law and courses taught by Professor Daniel Farber who is an expert in this realm. In addition, the Berkeley Law community is at the forefront of supporting young leaders who are implementing sustainable development ideas that address economic growth, social justice, and the environment. Berkeley Law has everything I am looking for in a graduate school program, exposure to the political, social, and economic forces that shape the law, and the opportunity to gain practical experience through an excellent Environmental Law Clinic. I also recognize the intersectionality between climate justice and social justice, and at Berkeley Law there is the perfect environment to brainstorm sustainable solutions for future iterations of environmental law and policies.

Appendix I: Academic Addenda Samples

Sample One: Being First Gen & Working Throughout College

I would like the Admissions Committee to give greater weight to my grades from the second half of my undergraduate career than my cumulative undergraduate GPA. As a first-generation college student, I struggled transitioning into my first-year of college without the necessary academic and financial resources to navigate an institution of higher education. I began working during my first year of college out of financial necessity, which took a toll on my first-year grades. This led me to seek a peer network and faculty mentorship support, leading to an upward academic trajectory as reflected in my transcript. I learned to balance being a full-time student, an active student leader, while working two to three jobs for 30-40 hours a week to make ends meet. Despite this, I graduated with cum laude honors and secured competitive positions and fellowships post-graduation, a better indication of my future promise as a law student.

Sample Two: Family Experiencing Bankruptcy & Falling Sick

In 2011, less than a year before I started my first semester of college at the University of Texas, my mother filed for bankruptcy. Our home was in foreclosure, and my mother's car had been repossessed. My mother was the head of the household, and her salary as a teacher in the Dallas Public Schools System (DPS) was constantly decreasing. As a result of the financial hardships that my family experienced, I spent my entire undergraduate education working multiple jobs to provide for myself and assist my mother financially back home in Dallas. There were times that I worked 2-3 student positions simultaneously to make ends meet. Due to my financial circumstances, I was unable to devout all of my time to my studies, and as a result, this negatively impacted my undergraduate GPA.

In the Fall 2014 term, I was diagnosed with an upper respiratory tract infection that required me to spend time in the emergency room at the University of Texas Hospital. I was ill for 2-3 weeks, and moved back home to Dallas with my mother as a result of my illness. I had to request extensions on all of my academic work and final examinations, and during this term, my GPA suffered. After recovering and moving back to campus, I did my best to catch up on my studies, but this was still challenging because of my financial circumstances.

In the Fall of 2016, things changed for my family. My mother started a new role within DPS that paid her more money, and I secured a contingent position with the University Health System as a Behavior Therapist, which paid enough for me to resign from both of my other positions. This gave me more time to devout to my education, and that term I earned a 4.0 GPA. Though my overall undergraduate GPA is lower, my performance does demonstrate my tenacity and persistence, which I have upheld despite facing multiple barriers. By the time that I attended graduate school for Social Work, I was in a much better space mentally, emotionally, and financially. As a graduate student, I earned an overall 3.9 GPA while working as a Graduate Student Instructor, and a Social Work Intern both at the University of Texas's Child Advocacy Law Clinic and Southwest Counseling Solutions in Austin. My training in Social Work taught me the importance of practicing self-care while working toward a professional degree. As a result, I believe that my graduate degree performance is a more accurate reflection of the kind of student I am and my ability to handle rigorous coursework.

Sample Three: Being First Gen & Struggling First Semester

As a first-generation college student, I began college completely unaware of how to properly navigate higher education. In addition, there were various circumstances (including financial hardship experienced by my family) back home that distracted me from school. This reality led to me working full-time while simultaneously trying to balance schoolwork and being a student. Not surprisingly, by the end of my first semester I had a 1.9 GPA. Consequently, I was placed on academic probation. Following this semester however, my grades had an upward trajectory. I consistently made mostly A's and B's and I was placed on the dean's list numerous times. I also maintained a GPA in academic good standing for the remainder of my undergraduate studies. Thus, my first semester grades (and the detrimental impact they have had on my overall GPA) are not an appropriate indication of my academic ability.

Sample Four: Being First Gen & Commuting Home Regularly

When I sat down in Chemistry class on my first day at college, I was woefully unprepared for higher education. As a first-generation college student from the underfunded public school system of Wilcox County, Alabama, I had no idea what I was getting myself into. And it showed. During my first three semesters, I struggled to the tune of a 2.25 cumulative GPA. I failed to develop proper study skills, lost all confidence in my academic abilities, and felt too ashamed to ask for help. At the same time, I had been commuting almost 14 hours every weekend back home. I had never been away from my family and because of the things shared in my personal statement, I was constantly worrying about my younger sister. I thought that I could study on the bus and spend as much time as I could with my family throughout the weekend but quickly realized this regular commute only amplified my struggles. I finally hit rock bottom and realized that a change needed to be made. At that point, my advisor introduced me to an academic counselor with whom I committed to weekly meetings to revamp my study habits and better position myself for academic success. I also realized that things back home had also become stable enough to the point where I wouldn't come home as often.

Although I put myself in a poor position at the start of my undergraduate career, with the help of key mentors and my family, I learned how to pull myself out. Beginning in the fall of my junior year, I never missed a meeting with my academic counselor and obtained a cumulative GPA exceeding 3.30 over my final two years in college. In my last semester, I achieved my best grades yet with a 3.43 GPA, demonstrating an upward academic trajectory.

186

While I recognize that my GPA may not be the most competitive, I am not the same student who naively stumbled into a Chemistry class in 2015. I am also not the same kid who couldn't stop worrying about what might happen back home. Following graduation, I have carried my improved work ethic into the workplace as a paralegal in the U.S. Attorney's Office for the Southern District of Alabama. This experience may not be as quantifiable as my undergraduate GPA struggles, but my enhanced writing, public speaking, and reasoning skills give me the confidence to succeed in law school.

Sample Five: Having an Undiagnosed Learning Disability

I know that my GPA is not indicative of my talents and ability to overcome any situation. Nevertheless, let me explain the reason for my poor academic performance. Not only did I start off school with a learning disadvantage that I did not discover until my early 40's, but my second semester of junior year of college my father had his first major heart attack. As a resul of being the oldest in my family, I subsequently had to take on several responsibilities including looking after my two younger siblings. So, I started working full-time to help provide for the family while I simultaneously tried to focus on being the first child to graduate from college. While assisting my parents financially and helping my baby sister complete high school and apply for college, some of my grades did slip. As a result, I was placed on academic probation. Fortunately, however, I did end up turning things around somewhat, however I ran out of time to significantly improve my GPA. For the aforementioned reasons, I believe that my undergraduate GPA from nearly two decades ago is not an accurate reflection of who I am likely to be today as a student.

Appendix J: LSAT Addenda Samples

Sample One: An 11-point increase over multiple exams

I took the September 2018 LSAT and received a score of 146. Prior to this exam I experienced the passing of my paternal grandfather. I was responsible for managing funeral arrangements transnationally because my family's undocumented status prevented them from traveling to Oaxaca. I underestimated how much of an impact this would have on my LSAT studying. I recognized that this score was not indicative of my abilities, so I regrouped and prepared for the June 2019 test. My increased score of 152 on this exam was a result of prioritizing my exam prep and adjusting my study strategies. Much like my persistence to improve and balance multiple responsibilities in college, I applied that diligence to increase my score to a 157 on the November 2021 exam, a stronger indication of my abilities to succeed in law school.

Sample Two: Improving after taking the test cold turkey

On my first two LSAT attempts, I took the test blindly with no prior preparation. That was a mistake and resulted in me scoring a 140 twice. Subsequently, I overstudied and was burnt out by the time I got to the actual test day. This led to the score of 139. Finally, upon taking my most recent LSAT exam, I was able to relax and utilize tools that helped me perform in a manner more reflective of my performance on practice tests. My 156 represents a 17-point increase from my lowest score and is the best indicator of my future performance in law school. This score is the result of more effective studying, pacing, and relaxation techniques.

Sample Three: Score decreased significantly

The first time I took the LSAT my score was 134. During this time, I did not have enough time to study or resources to get help. At the time, I only studied for one month. The second time I took the LSAT my score increased by 17 points. In order for me to receive the 151, I spent 7 months of studying with tutors and utilized a LSAT prep course. If it were not for the technical difficulties and taking my test a day and three hours late, I believe I would have scored even higher. Because of the technical difficulties I took the exam in February as well.

189

Unfortunately, there were a 13-point decrease between January and February. On the February test day I was not feeling my best mentally and physically, which played a significant role on my test. While feeling ill, I was also going through personal issues that affected me mentally and was not able to fully focus on the exam. To make matters worse, I also was not able to take the exam at home because of technical difficulties and had to ask family members for help securing a testing area with good Wi-Fi. For the aforementioned reasons, I ask that the admissions committee place the most weight on the 151 that I scored and use that as a tool to determine my ability to succeed in law school.

Sample Four: Taking the exam after experiencing a death in the family

I received a 139 on the December 2021 LSAT. I prepped for six months and was testing in the 150s prior to the test. I had previously taken the LSAT and scored a 153 in 2012. Unfortunately, this score was no longer valid. About 20 minutes prior to the test beginning, I noticed I had numerous missed calls from various family members. When I was able to get in contact with my grandmother, she informed me that my grandfather passed away. It was too late for me to withdraw from the test. So, I took the test with a veiled perspective, constantly reiterating the fact that I did not get to say goodbye before he transitioned. I believe my February 2022 LSAT score of a 155 is a more accurate indicator of my potential to succeed in law school. By the time I retook the test, although still grieving, I was able to better focus on the task at hand. This is what I believe led to the recent 16-point increase in my score.

Appendix K: Sample Character & Fitness Questions

While every school is different, typically, the two kinds of character and fitness disclosures that applicants have to make fall within one of two categories: criminal or academic / professional disclosures. Below is an example of what schools may ask you to disclose.

Criminal Disclosures:

Have you committed any offense against the law, including any crime, misdemeanor, petty offense, ordinance violation, warning, alcohol or drug-related offense, traffic violation within the past five years (excluding parking tickets), traffic violation involving drugs or alcohol at any time, or other violation of any law, statute, or regulation that you ever have been under investigation for, taken into custody and questioned about, accused formally or informally of, charged with, arrested for, cited for, convicted of, or pled guilty or no contest to.

Academic Disclosures:

Are there any disciplinary incidents from any of your academic institutions or places of employment, including warnings, disciplinary actions, probations, suspensions, requests from the school for you to resign or take time off, expulsions, honor or student conduct code violations, or violations of residential or dorm policies such as those related to alcohol or controlled substances.

192

Appendix L: Character & Fitness Addenda
Samples

Sample One: Charged with disorderly conduct

Sometime around 2012, I was issued a summons for disorderly conduct. At the time I was 17 years old; an officer pulled up while myself and two other individuals were sitting on a vehicle. The officer asked for I.D. which I provided, yet the others were told to "walk." I later filed a complaint against the officer considering the other individuals indicated that they were on probation and bail respectively. The judge stated it was a waste of the court's time and issued an adjournment in contemplation of dismissal (ACD). I had no prior or future contact with law enforcement, the ACD terms were met, and the matter was dismissed after six months.

Sample Two: Charged with burglary

On June 14, 2009, I was charged with burglary with a battery therein and criminal mischief in Orlando, Florida. At the time, I was in my twenties, the mother of a new-born, a full-time student, and working full-time. Also around that time, my husband had cheated on me, so needless to say he and I were going through a very rough separation. Although I still lived in the house with my husband at the time, I was in the process of moving things out because I had just caught my husband on the phone with his mistress. That night, things escalated as we argued so I decided to leave. As I was getting the rest of my things I was locked outside the house by my husband. Despite me having a key, he blocked the door so that I could not get in to either the front or back door. In an attempt to catch his attention to let me back in, I tapped the window with my keys and my hand accidentally went through the glass, breaking it. I had no idea that the glass on the window was so thin or that a simple tap would have that result. It was definitely not my intent to break the window. When I noticed that I was severely injured by my hand going through the window and getting cut by the glass, I simply left. However, I did not realize that as a result of that window break, my husband had called the cops. In what I think was his anger towards me for confronting him for cheating, he blatantly lied to the

194

officers about who I was and what I did as perhaps a way to punish or hurt me. Since I was not at the house to explain what happened to the cops when they arrived, the charges were filed against me.

Completely unaware of the whole situation, a few days later, I got a call from a Sheriff friend of mine who notified me that he had a warrant for my arrest. Unbeknownst to me as to why, I quickly went to the Sheriff's office and had him take me in to discuss the charges. After I received a court date, I hired an attorney. During the investigation it was revealed that the officers at the scene were not told that I lived at the property, owned a key, and was listed as a tenant on the lease. **Due to these facts, the judge considered the charges against me to be inappropriate, and my case was immediately dismissed. I sealed and expunged that record soon after the dismissal.**

Sample Three: Threatening a roommate

During the spring semester of my freshman year, I was involved in a verbal altercation with a former friend through text message. We went back and forth a couple times until the conversation escalated to the point where a physical threat was made. This text message exchange resulted in me being placed on probation until I completed a total of 120 hours of community service.

Prior to this unfortunate mishap I had not been in any trouble in or outside of school and was on track to finish out the school year on a positive path. That incident was an eye opener for me, and I have made it a goal to *never* putting myself in such a position again. I removed myself from hanging around the people that assisted in the events leading to that incident and have stayed away from anyone and anything that seemed like trouble or drama.

Though I am not proud of my actions, I am thankful for the experience; it truly helped me to grow up and let go of the high school mentality and immaturity that I was holding on to. I am glad I could use that incident as a lesson because I was able to keep it in the back of my mind as a reminder of the consequences that come with making poor decisions. I successfully completed my community service hours by the fall of my sophomore year and finished undergrad without any other disciplinary infractions.

Sample Four: Traffic Offenses

I would like to address the following citations on my driving record in my continued efforts to be as transparent as I can be. Since my most recent traffic offense, which occurred nearly a decade ago, I have been deliberate about following all traffic laws and avoiding any future citations. While I can't erase my traffic history, I can say with confidence that the driver I am today is very different from the driver I was ten years ago.

Toll Infraction	12/22/2011	TR- FAILURE TO PAY TOLL Statute: 316.1001 No Degree - Infraction
Civil Traffic Infraction	09/24/2011	TR- UNLAWFUL SPEED Statute: 316.183(2) No Degree - Infraction
Civil Traffic Infraction	7/27/2010	TR- UNLAWFUL SPEED Statute: 316.189(2) No Degree - Infraction TR- CERT OF REGISTRATION POSSESS REQ Statute: 320.0605 No Degree - Infraction TR- INSURANCE REQUIRED PROOF OF PIP AND PDL Statute: 316.646(1) No Degree - Infraction

Appendix M: Applicant Profile Grids (How to Find Them)

To find applicant profile grids, follow these steps:

- Go to LSAC.org →
  - Click on "Choosing A Law School" →
  - Select "ABA Approved Law Schools" →
  - Choose "View all schools"→
  - (select the school) →
  - Scroll to bottom of school profile and see if there is an applicant profile grid at the very bottom of the screen

Appendix N: Application Status Check Sample Email

Subject: Application Status Inquiry

"Good Morning / Afternoon,

Please pardon my interruption. My name is _____ and my LSAC number is _____ . I am writing to inquire about the status of my application. I can't imagine how busy you all may be right now, but is there any way that you may be able to share when I may expect to receive a decision? I really appreciate you all taking the time to review my file.

Warm regards,
{Insert Name}"

Appendix O: LOCI Sample Email

Subject: Continued Interest

Body:
Dear {insert admissions' person's title and last name},

My name is _____ , and I am writing to express my continued interest in attending your institution should a seat become available. If you have any questions or concerns please don't hesitate to contact me at {insert phone number}.

I appreciate you taking the time to reconsider my file and I am hopeful about the possibility of being able to matriculate at your school this fall!

Warm regards,
{Insert name}

www.ingramcontent.com/pod-product-compliance
Lightning Source LLC
Chambersburg PA
CBHW080238270326
41926CB00020B/4290